Picture Stories

Language and Literacy Activities for Beginners

FRED LIGON

ELIZABETH TANNENBAUM

WITH CAROL RICHARDSON RODGERS

In Association with
The Experiment in International Living

Illustrations by Fred Ligon

Longman

Picture Stories

Longman, 10 Bank Street, White Plains, N.Y. 10606

Associated companies:
Longman Group Ltd., London
Longman Cheshire Pty., Melbourne
Longman Paul Pty., Auckland
Copp Clark Pitman, Toronto

Distributed in the United Kingdom by Longman Group
Ltd., Longman House, Burnt Mill, Harlow, Essex CM20
2JE, England and by associated companies, branches,
and representatives throughout the world.

The authors are very grateful to our friends and colleagues in the U.S. Department of State, Bureau of Refugee Affairs, Refugee Education Training Programs who have given their support and shared their ideas, and to the refugees who tried out our activities while preparing for U.S. resettlement in the refugee camps in Thailand, Indonesia, the Philippines, the Sudan and Eastern Europe.

Special thanks go to: the original group of supervisors and teachers on Galang; Kathleen Corey, Kay Stark, Patrick Moran and Steven Epstein, who made valuable comments on the manuscript; Orawan Kongrawd, Teerawat Lungtaisong, Therdsak Puggarana, and the staff of Projects in International Development and Training at the Experiment in International Living for their support and technical assistance in the preparation of the manuscript; Claude Pepin, Al Hoel, Don Batchelder, Helju Batchelder and Lois Purdham for their support and encouragement; Joanne Dresner for helping us develop the format of the book; Lynn Savage, our editor and friend, who made working on the final drafts of the book a lot of fun; and Peter, Marcus, and Andrew Falion for putting up with it and us.

Executive editor: Joanne Dresner
Development editor: K. Lynn Savage
Production editor: Helen B. Ambrosio
Text design adaptation: José Almaquer
Cover design: José Almaquer
Cover illustration/photo: Fred Ligon
Text art: Fred Ligon

Library of Congress Cataloging in Publication Data

Ligon, Fred.
    Picture stories: language and literacy activities for beginners/
Fred Ligon, Elizabeth Tannenbaum, with Carol Richardson Rodgers; in
association with the Experiment in International Living;
illustrations by Fred Ligon.
      p. cm.
    ISBN 0-8013-0366-4
    1. English language—Textbooks for foreign speakers.
I. Tannenbaum, Elizabeth. II. Rodgers, Carol Richardson.
III. Experiment in International Living. IV. Title.
PE1128.L464 1990
428.2'4—dc20   89-13827
                                 CIP

19 20 21 22 - CRS - 05 04 03 02 01

Contents

Introduction

Picture Stories: Language and Literacy Activities for Beginners consists of 16 picture stories for adult and young adult students living in or outside the U.S. who have limited English ability and little familiarity with U.S. cultural practices. The stories are most appropriate for students with basic literacy skills and with survival ESL needs.

Told through a sequence of 10 pictures, each story deals with a particular cultural topic. The topics are presented through situations and everyday events that might happen to persons adjusting to life in the U.S. The characters in the stories know very little English, have minimal literacy skills and have little knowledge of American culture. The experiences of the characters allow students to analyze their own situations, evaluate options and even anticipate potential problems before they happen. The humor in the stories makes them fun to read and encourages discussion.

The book consists of two parts: 16 student units and a Teacher's Notes section with separate notes for each student unit. Before beginning to work with the units:

- Look through the table of contents. Read the story titles; choose a story based on the needs of the class.
- Look through the exercises in the chosen story.
- Read through the Teacher's Notes at the back of the book.

Student Unit Exercises

All student units follow the same format and include exercises for listening, speaking, reading and writing. No unit is dependent on any other, so a teacher may select any unit related to a chosen topic. However, all the stories take place in the same town. By using the map on the inside back cover and finding the location of each story, students can think of the characters as part of one community.

The exercises can be used with a variety of current ESL methodologies. Exercises include options for work with the whole class, small groups, pairs or individuals. The variety of exercises also addresses various learning styles and includes teacher-directed as well as student-directed exercises.

Talk about the Pictures. Then Listen to the Story.

A series of pictures, which read from left to right and from top to bottom (just as the pages of a book are read), provides the stimulus for oral language. These pictures establish a context for the later literacy work by giving students the oral vocabulary and the needed cultural background information to understand the text. They create a motivation for reading because of student interest and involvement in the stories.

Procedure: Students look at the pictures and describe them. Students may be able to produce only a single word description. Accept several students' responses, and then create a clear statement. For example (Unit 1, 1/2 Cup):

> Teacher: What do you see in Frame 1?
> Student 1: man
> Student 2: clothes
> Student 3: stairs
> Teacher: Right. The man takes his clothes downstairs.

As students generate vocabulary and possibly sentences for each frame, write their words on the board. Exposure to the written language at this point helps students connect print to oral language and helps prepare them for the literacy exercises in the rest of the unit.

After the students have generated language for each frame, they are ready to listen to the entire story. Tell the story, expanding on the vocabulary generated by the students, or have the class tell the story together, incorporating previously generated vocabulary. Guide the telling of the story with questions such as the following for Unit 1, 1/2 Cup:

- What's happening in Frame 1?
- What is the man doing in Frame 2?
- What does the box say in Frame 4?
- Where is the man in Frame 10?

The story can be told several times with teacher and students working together to refine the language. After adequate oral practice with the whole group, have students work in pairs to describe each frame. At this point accuracy is not essential.

Variations

Comprehension: After the story has been told, check student comprehension by giving commands which require only nonverbal responses, for example, "Point to the *man*.", "Put an X on the *soap*.", "Circle the *clothes*."

Frame by Frame: Make a copy of the story and cut it into frames. Before students see the story in the book, give groups of students one frame at a time. After each frame, ask, "What is happening?" "What do you think will happen next?"

Action Sequence: Many of the stories include a sequence of steps that lead to a specific end result. Some examples are: making a pay phone call, operating a washing machine, taking a bus. Using pictures or props, present the language to describe the steps in the activity. For example, demonstrate putting clothes in the washing machine. Have students follow your directions and then give each other the commands.

Number the Pictures in Order. Then Tell the Story.

This exercise focuses on sequencing skills and on the concept that stories have a beginning, a middle and an end.

Procedure: Point out that frame number 1 has already been numbered. Have students work individually or in pairs to number the rest of the pictures in order. Check the answers by reading aloud the numbers from top to bottom in each column, by having individual students read aloud the numbers or by having students in pairs or small groups compare their answers. Then have the whole class, small groups or pairs tell the story.

Variations

Scrambled Pictures: Make copies of the picture story and cut them into 10 frames. Give each group of students a cut-up picture story to put in order.

Narration: Narrate the story and have students number the frames in the order read. This variation works especially well with stories that have a possibility of more than one correct order.

Match the Picture with the Sentence.

This exercise focuses on connecting oral language to written language: both the previously practiced oral language as well as the language that the teacher has written on the board based on the students' telling of the story.

Procedure: First do the example sentence with the whole class. Then have students draw a line from the picture frame to the sentence that relates to that frame. Prepare less literate classes for this exercise by writing the sentences on the board or on large strips of paper and then having the class as a whole read the sentences before asking students to work on their own. Have students check their work in pairs or by having individual students read aloud the print that matches each of the frames.

Variations

Matching Pairs: Write one sentence (or key word) for each frame on a 3x5 card. Cut up the picture story and paste each frame on a card. Have students match each picture frame with the appropriate sentence (key word). Divide students in pairs or small groups. Give each group a set of the 3 x 5 cards. Then have the students place the cards in scrambled order face down on a table. Have students take turns turning over two cards at a time to find a match. As the students turn over the cards, they can orally describe the picture or read aloud the sentence. The student with the most matches is the winner.

Listen.

The listening exercises focus on real communication situations such as understanding addresses or phone numbers.

Procedure: Teach the vocabulary in the exercise by following the suggestions in the Teacher's Notes for each unit. Read aloud the script from the Teacher's Notes section. Do number one with the whole class. Show students how to indicate (circle, write, number) the correct answer. Then have students listen and complete the exercise. Have students check their answers in pairs, with the whole class, by taking turns writing the correct answers on the board, or by taking the role of the teacher and reading the answers to the class.

Variations

Change the script. After doing the exercise once by the script, change the script, for example: read item c instead of item a, and do the activity again in order to practice with different vocabulary.

Play the Game.

The games put the language into real-life situations. They shift the focus away from the teacher and help students learn from each other. They encourage cooperation and help students develop the skill of completing a task on their own.

Procedure: First teach the relevant vocabulary on the page. Ask students to circle any words they don't know. Then have students work in pairs or small groups to decide the meaning of any new words by matching each of the words with one of the frames from the picture story. For words not used in the picture story, make classroom visuals that illustrate the word and have students match the visual to the word card. For common sight words (such as Danger, Emergency, Help Wanted), make large word cards and post them around the room so that students will constantly be exposed to important sight words. Have students explain where they might see these words outside of class. Next draw the game board on the chalkboard. Ask two students to come to the front of the room. Demonstrate the game rules written in the student text at the beginning of each game. Have the two students follow your directions. Be sure to point out start, finish, the direction of the play and where to write the answers. Finally, divide students into pairs and give each pair the materials needed to play the game:

- Markers: Use items such as bingo chips, small pieces of paper or bottle caps. Each pair needs two markers of different colors for the board games and two different color sets of five markers for three-in-a-row.
- Dice: Provide each pair of students with one die.

Circle T for True or F for False.

Students use their knowledge of the story and their developing reading comprehension skills to make deductions and to draw conclusions. All the words and the sentence structures in this exercise have been seen previously. In this exercise students encounter the familiar words and structures in new arrangements.

Procedure: Write the first statement on the board with T F by it. Read it to the class. Ask students if the statement is true or false. Show students how to indicate the correct answer. Then have students read and complete the exercise. After they have finished, have students check their work in small groups or as a large class by having individual students read the sentences aloud and tell if the statement is true or false.

Variations

Students rewrite the false statements to make them true.

Fill in the Blanks.

This exercise gives students the first opportunity to write what they have already seen in print in the previous exercises.

Procedure: Do the first blank together as a large class. Then have students work individually or in pairs to fill in the remaining blanks with an appropriate word. Initially students may need to copy words from other places in the text or work together to write the words.

Variations

Copying: For less literate students, write the words that are used to fill in the blanks on the board in random order. Have students choose the appropriate word for each blank and copy it in the appropriate place.

Dictation: Read the Fill-in-the-Blanks passage aloud; have students fill in the blanks with the words they hear.

Grammar Focus: Write the Fill-in-the-Blanks passage on the board, leaving blanks for different parts of speech, such as verbs and pronouns.

Write the Story.

This final exercise in each of the units is a culmination of the work in the previous exercises. This exercise reinforces the previous work with vocabulary, sentence word order, syntax and sequencing. For the first time, students write complete sentences in a narrative form. However, the focus is on expressing ideas and not on grammatical accuracy.

Procedure

Key Words: Review the key words by having students match the words with the picture story frames.

Additional Words: Have students work with a partner (or with the entire class) to write additional words that they remember from the story. Assist students in writing words they cannot spell.

Write the Story: Have students use the key words, additional words they have identified and the first and last picture frames to cue their writing of the story. Work with individual students, asking clarification questions and helping the students spell words they are having trouble putting into print. Do not demand perfect grammar or a sentence for each frame. Some students will initially be able to write only a few words or only partial sentences.

Variations

Student-to-Student Correction: Have students read each other's writing and help make corrections.

Class Correction: Choose sentences with common errors from several students' compositions. Write these sentences anonymously on the board and have the class work together to make the corrections.

Teacher's Notes.

Following the student text are detailed notes to the teacher for each unit. These notes provide:

1. Background information (subject, situation, cultural notes).
2. Procedures for setting up each exercise and answer keys.
3. Suggestions for expansion exercises divided into vocabulary, grammar, listening, speaking, reading and writing.
4. Closing exercises which include map reading activities, role-plays and critical-thinking questions.

A. Talk about the pictures. Then listen to the story.

B. Number the pictures in order. Then tell the story.

C. Match the picture with the sentence.

1.

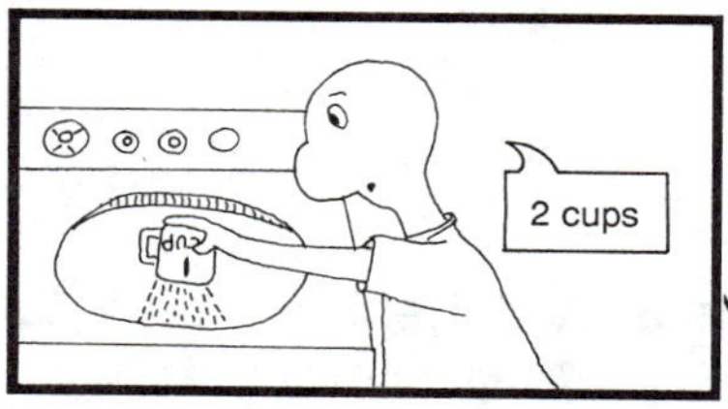

a. The man puts the dirty clothes in the washing machine.

2.

b. There is a lot of soap on the stairs.

3.

c. The man pours 2 cups of soap into the washing machine.

4.

d. The man reads the directions on the box.

5.

e. The man takes his clothes downstairs.

D. Match the picture with the word.

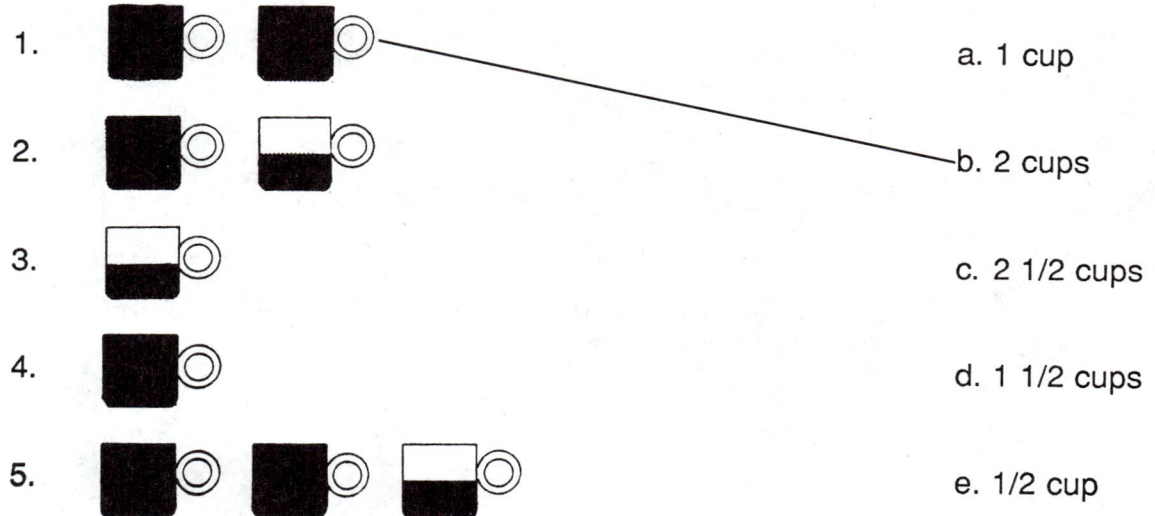

1.

a. 1 cup

2.

b. 2 cups

3.

c. 2 1/2 cups

4.

d. 1 1/2 cups

5.

e. 1/2 cup

E. You want to wash your clothes. Look at the words. Circle the words you don't know. Ask the meaning.

dirty clothes   soap   directions
washing machine   cup   bleach

F. **WASHING MACHINE GAME.** Play with a partner. One is A. One is B. Take turns. Throw one of the dice. Move your marker. Look at the picture. What is it?

Player A: Find the word in Box A. Put an X by the word.
Player B: Find the word in Box B. Put an X by the word.

The winner has the most X's.

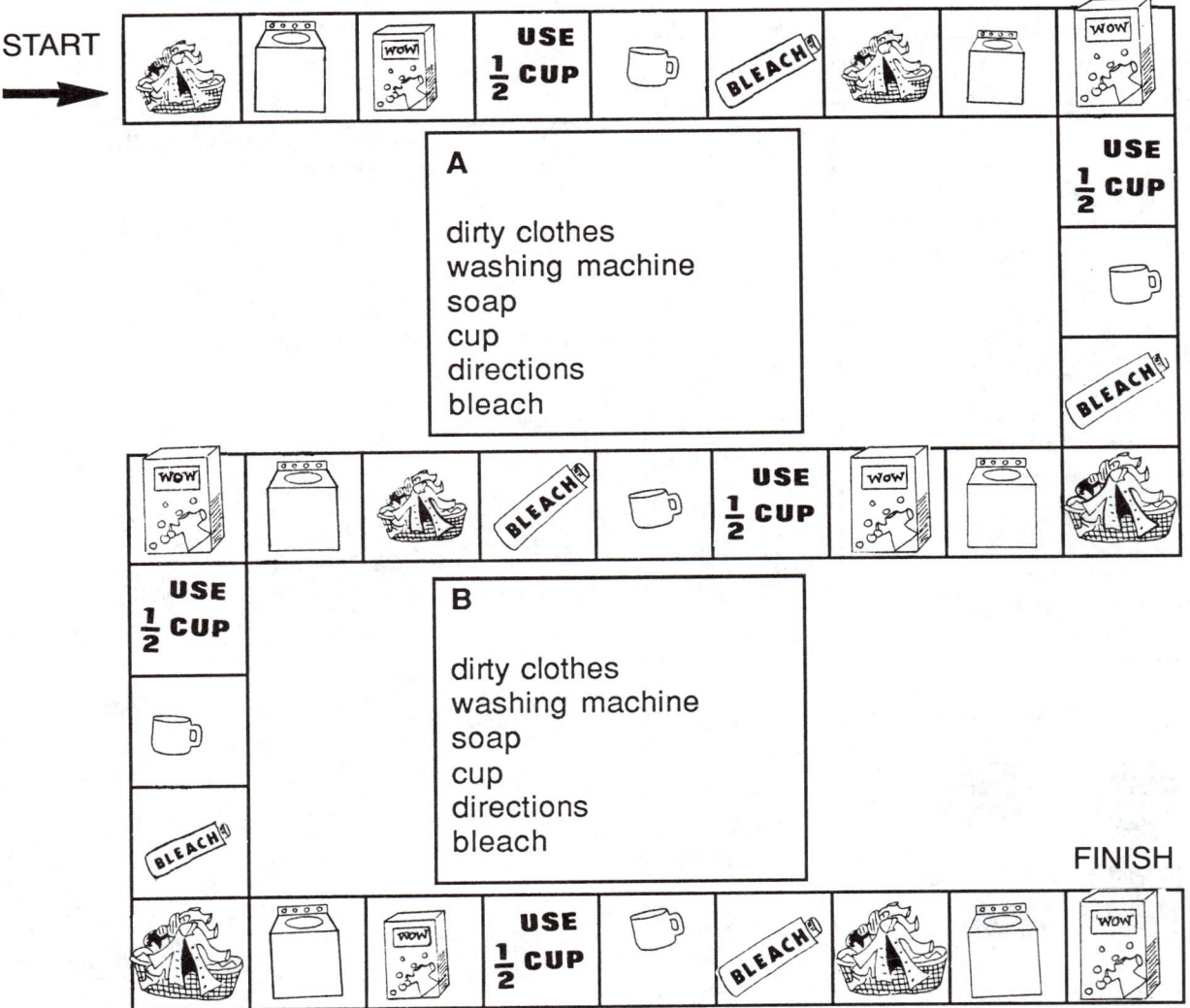

Note: A player can put more than one X next to each word. Players only go around once. A player who reaches the finish box waits for the other player to complete the game.

G. Circle T for True or F for False.

1. The man takes his clothes upstairs.   T   F

2. The man uses 3 cups of soap.   T   F

3. The man pours the soap into the box.   T   F

4. The man picks up the box of soap.   T   F

5. The man uses too much soap.   T   F

6. The man sits downstairs.   T   F

7. The man reads the directions.   T   F

H. Fill in the blanks.

A man wants to wash his clothes. Look at the story. Tell him what to do.

1. _____ downstairs.

2. _____ the clothes in the washing machine.

3. _____ the box of soap.

4. _____ the directions. _____ only 1/2 cup.

5. _____ the soap into a cup.

6. _____ the soap into the washing machine.

7. _____ down and _____ a newspaper.

Oh, no! Too much soap!

I. Write the story.

Look at these words from the story.

clothes   soap   cup
washing machine   read the directions   too much

Work with your teacher or a partner. Write other words you remember from the story.

_____

_____

Now write the story. Use the words to help you.

A. Talk about the pictures. Then listen to the story.

C. Match the picture with the word. Match the word with the sentence.

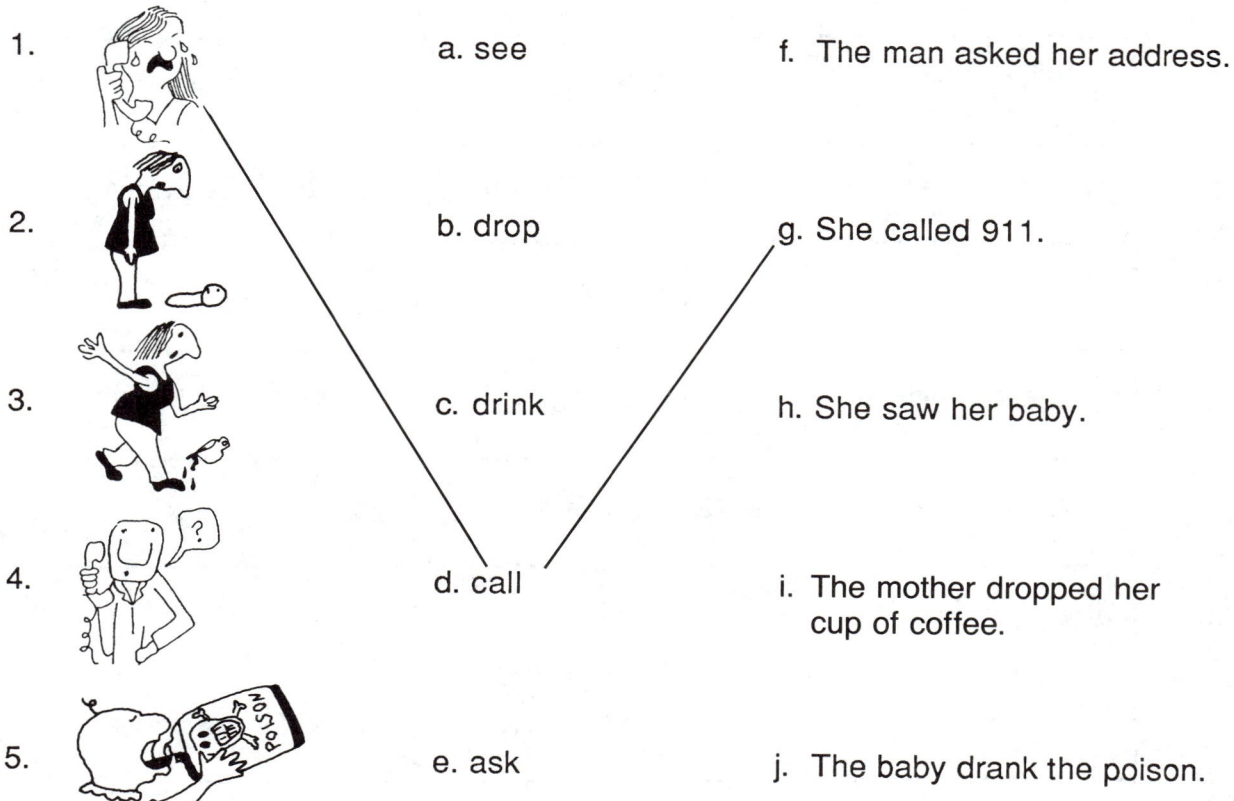

1.
2.
3.
4.
5.

a. see
b. drop
c. drink
d. call
e. ask

f. The man asked her address.
g. She called 911.
h. She saw her baby.
i. The mother dropped her cup of coffee.
j. The baby drank the poison.

D. Who do you call? Match the problem with the person. Match the person with the word.

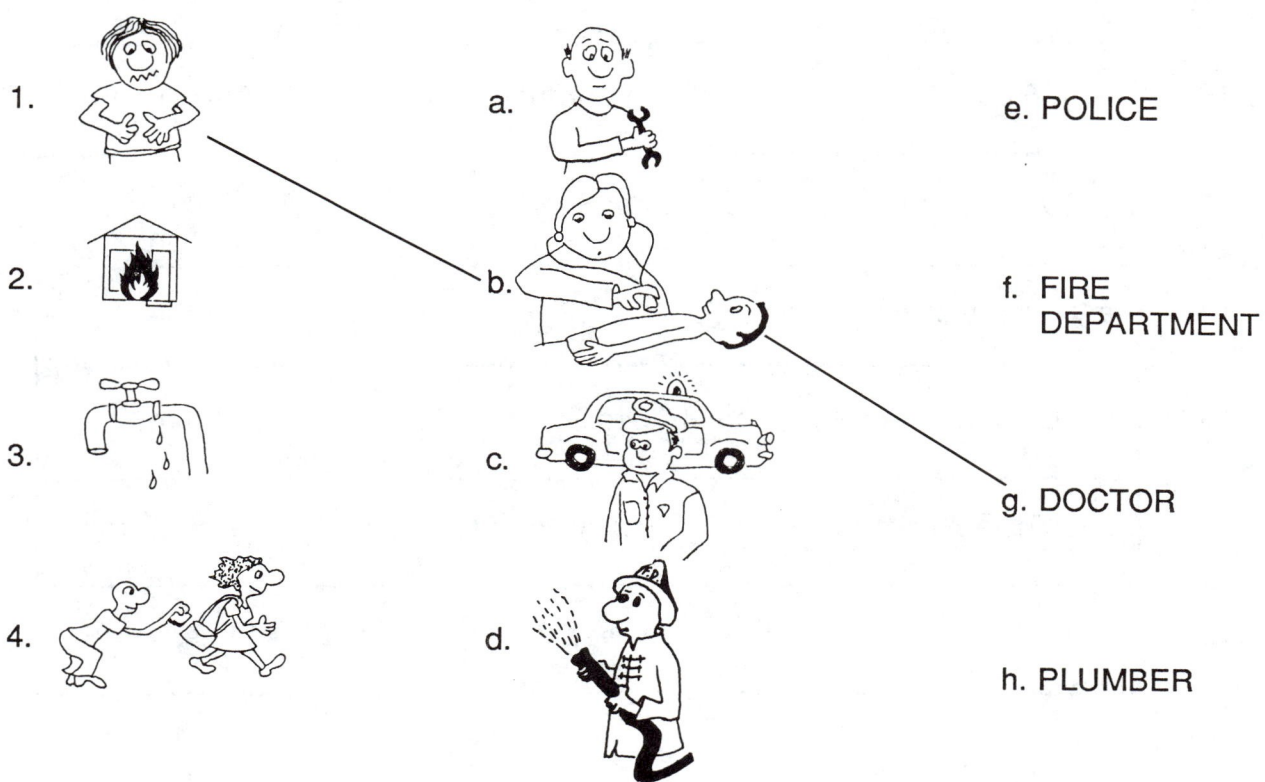

1.
2.
3.
4.

a.
b.
c.
d.

e. POLICE
f. FIRE DEPARTMENT
g. DOCTOR
h. PLUMBER

E. Listen to the teacher. Circle the address you hear.

1.	a. 33 D Street	b. 33 C Street	c. 33 B Street
2.	a. 14 Circle Street	b. 4D Circle Street	c. 40 Circle Street
3.	a. 16 16th Avenue	b. 60 16th Avenue	c. 6 16th Avenue
4.	a. 50A Ram Drive	b. 15 Ram Drive	c. 50 Ram Drive
5.	a. 20 14th Street	b. 24 14th Street	c. 4 14th Street
6.	a. 7 M Avenue	b. 7 Men Avenue	c. 7 N Avenue
7.	a. 15 Green Drive	b. 50 Green Drive	c. 55 Green Drive
8.	a. 10 Second Street	b. 10 Seventh Street	c. 10 Sixth Street
9.	a. 61 Man Street	b. 61 Mean Street	c. 61 Main Street
10.	a. 108 80th Street	b. 100 80th Street	c. 118 80th Street
11.	a. 90 First Street	b. 91 First Street	c. 19 First Street
12.	a. 3 Green Drive	b. 3 Clean Drive	c. 3 Mean Drive
13.	a. 40 Third Street	b. 44 Third Street	c. 4 Third Street
14.	a. 2 Seventh Street	b. 7 Seventh Street	c. 72 Seventh Street
15.	a. 13 A Street	b. 3 A Street	c. 33 A Street

F. Circle T for True or F for False.

1. The mother fell down.   T   F

2. The baby drank poison.   T   F

3. The woman called 411.   T   F

4. The woman dropped her cup of coffee.   T   F

5. The woman screamed.   T   F

6. The baby saw the poison.   T   F

7. The man asked, "What's your address?"   T   F

G. Fill in the blanks.

Yesterday a baby _____ a bottle of poison. He _____ the poison
                      1   2

and got sick. Then he _____ down. His mother walked into the room. She
                               3

_____ the baby. She _____ and _____ her cup of coffee.
     4   5   6

She _____ 911. A man _____, "What's the problem?" She said,
      7   8

"My baby _____ poison." The man asked, "What's your
             9

address?" She said, "My _____ is 33 B Street."
                         10

H. Write the story.

Look at these words from the story.

baby	sick	walk	address
poison	fall	scream	
drink	mother	call 911	

Work with your teacher or a partner. Write other words you remember from the story.

_____

_____

Now write the story. Use the words to help you.

Checkout Counter

A. Talk about the pictures. Then listen to the story.

B. Number the pictures in order. Then tell the story.

C. Match the picture to the sentence. Circle the correct word in each sentence.

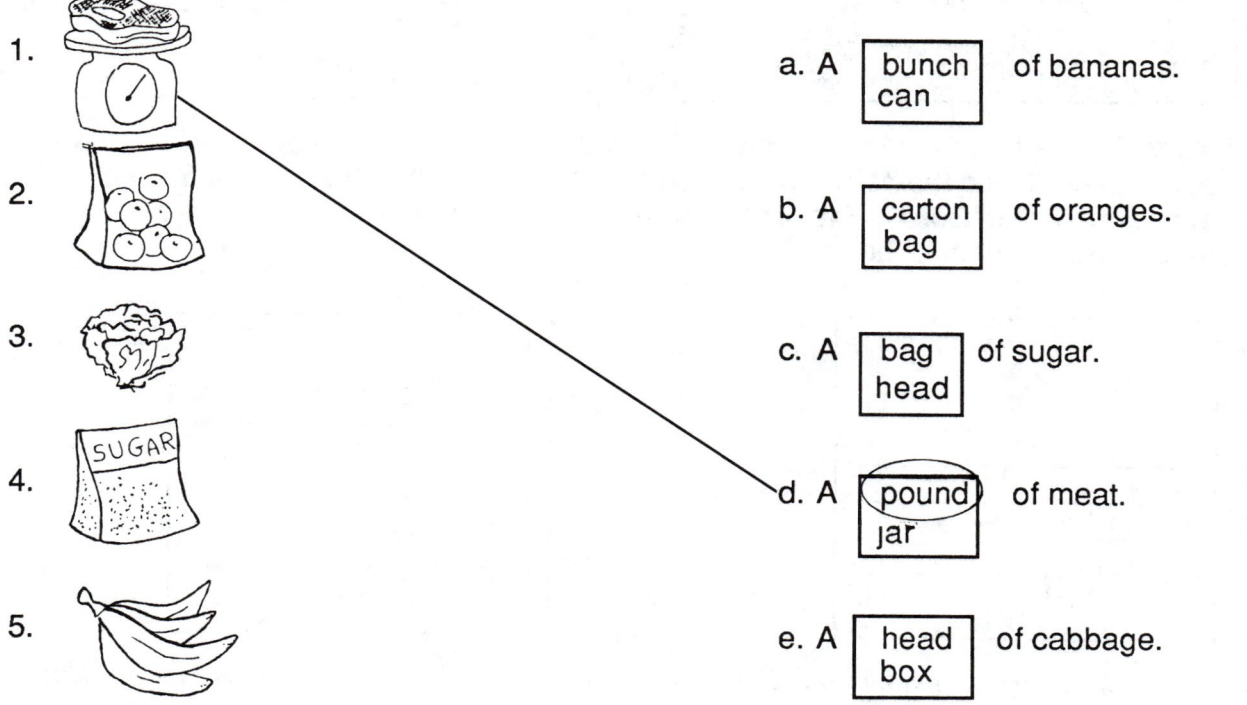

1.

2.

3.

4.

5.

6.

a. She buys a | carton / box | of eggs.

b. She puts down a | carton / jar | of coffee.

c. She pays for a | bottle / bunch | of juice.

d. She picks up a | box / bottle | of tea.

e. She puts down the | carton / can | of soup.

f. She buys a (bag) / can | of rice.

D. Match the picture with the sentence. Circle the correct word in each sentence.

1.

2.

3.

4.

5.

a. A | bunch / can | of bananas.

b. A | carton / bag | of oranges.

c. A | bag / head | of sugar.

d. A (pound) / jar | of meat.

e. A | head / box | of cabbage.

E. SHOPPING GAME. Look at the words on the board. Circle the words you don't know. Ask the meaning.

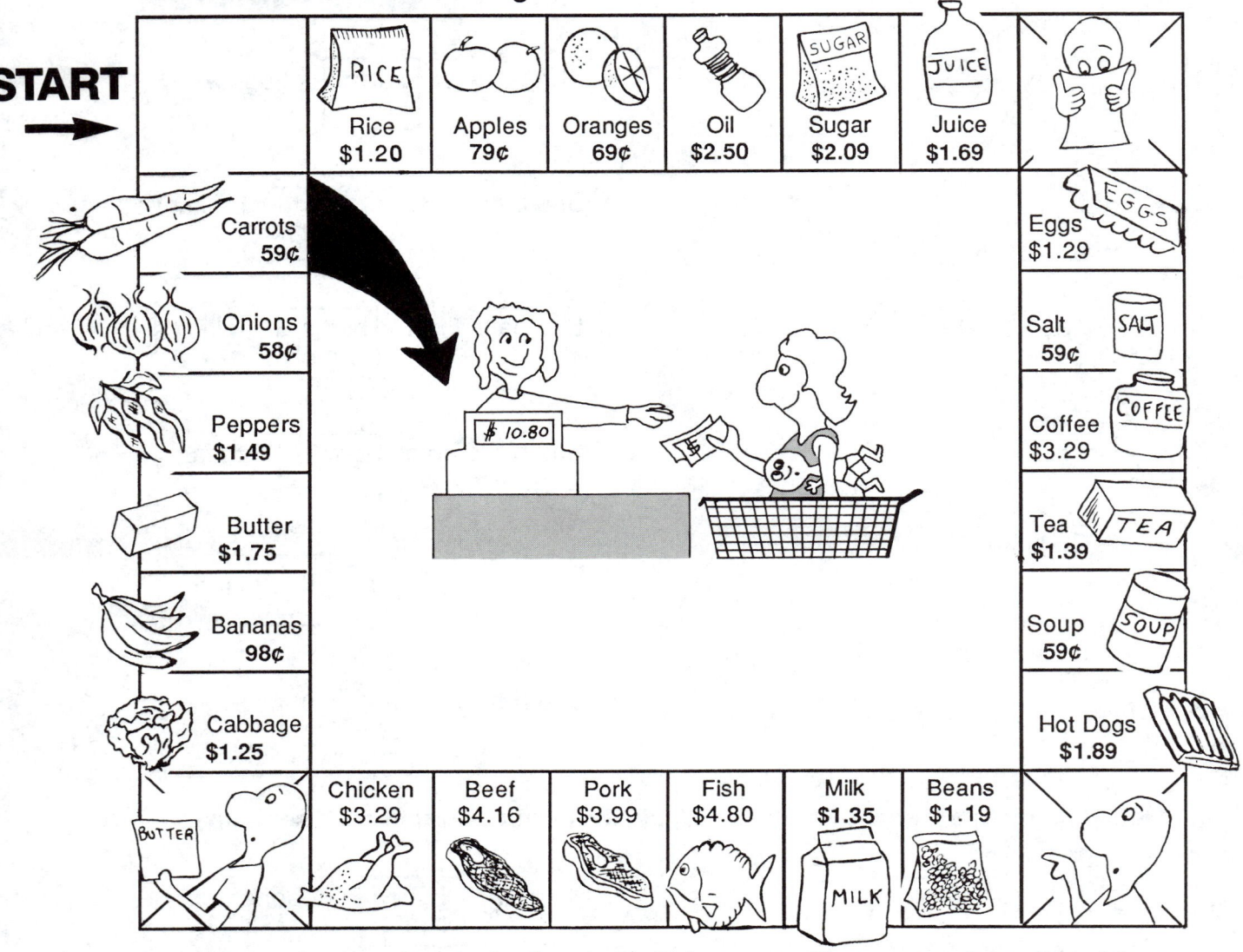

Play with a partner. One is A. One is B. Take turns. Throw one of the dice. Move your marker. Read the name of the food and the price. **Player A:** Write the food name and price in Box A. **Player B:** Write the food name and price in Box B. At the checkout counter, add the prices.

A	$
TOTAL	

B	$
TOTAL	

Note: The players continue throwing one of the dice, and recording items and prices, until they reach the checkout counter.

F. Circle T for True or F for False.

1. The woman has 2 babies in her shopping cart.   T   F

2. The woman is at the supermarket.   T   F

3. The woman puts her baby on the counter.   T   F

4. The woman pays for her baby.   T   F

5. The woman buys a carton of eggs.   T   F

6. The woman picks up her baby.   T   F

7. The woman pays for the food.   T   F

G. Fill in the blanks.

A woman is at the checkout counter in a supermarket. She's taking food out of her

shopping cart. She puts a _____ of milk, a _____ of tea and a
                              1   2

_____ of soup on the counter. She also puts a _____ of
      3   4

eggs, a _____ of juice, a _____ of rice and a _____ of
        5   6   7

coffee on the counter. Then she _____ her baby on the _____.
                                        8   9

The cashier is surprised. The woman is surprised, too. She asks, "Where's my

_____?" She picks up her baby and pays for the food.
      10

H. Write the story.
   Look at these words from the story.

woman	cashier	put	surprised
supermarket	shopping cart	baby	
checkout counter	pick up	pay for	

Work with your teacher or a partner. Write other words you remember from the story.

_____

_____

Now write the story. Use the words to help you.

Dr. Lee

A. Talk about the pictures. Then listen to the story.

B. Number the pictures in order. Then tell the story.

C. Match the picture with the sentence.

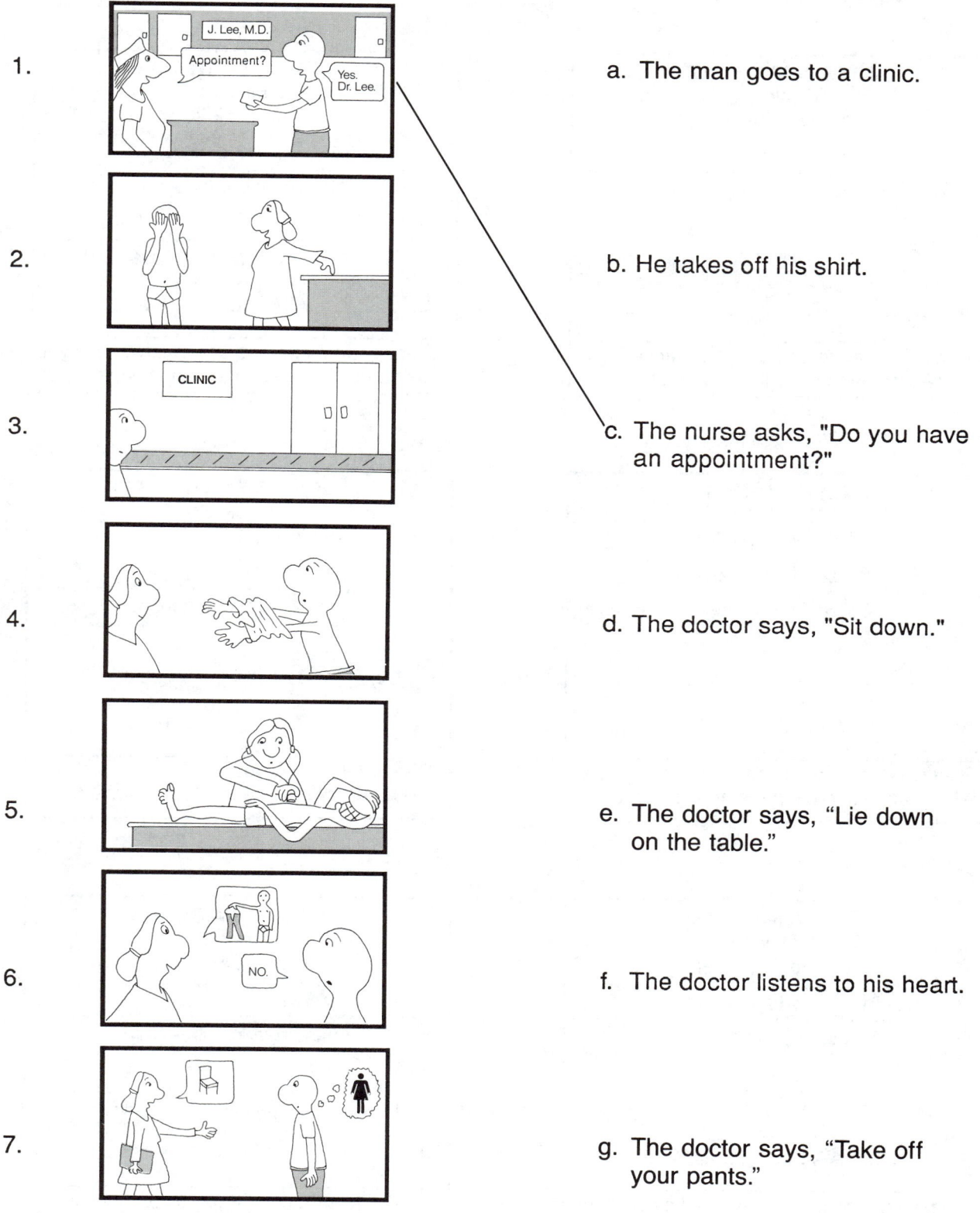

1.

a. The man goes to a clinic.

2.

b. He takes off his shirt.

3.

c. The nurse asks, "Do you have an appointment?"

4.

d. The doctor says, "Sit down."

5.

e. The doctor says, "Lie down on the table."

6.

f. The doctor listens to his heart.

7.

g. The doctor says, "Take off your pants."

D. Listen to the teacher. Write the day, date and time you hear on appointment card 1. Repeat with cards 2–6.

①

```
              JOHN N. SMITH, M.D.
                   8 Main St.
               Phone 259-7328
              Mr. E. Lee
..........................................................
              has an appointment on

..........................................................
     Day          Month          Date

At ............... A.M. ............. P.M. .............
_____
Please telephone one day in advance if you
will be unable to keep the appointment.
```

②

```
              JOHN N. SMITH, M.D.
                   8 Main St.
               Phone 259-7328
              Ms. B. Brown
..........................................................
              has an appointment on

..........................................................
     Day          Month          Date

At ............... A.M. ............. P.M. .............
_____
Please telephone one day in advance if you
will be unable to keep the appointment.
```

③

```
              JOHN N. SMITH, M.D.
                   8 Main St.
               Phone 259-7328
              Mr. P. Brown
..........................................................
              has an appointment on

..........................................................
     Day          Month          Date

At ............... A.M. ............. P.M. .............
_____
Please telephone one day in advance if you
will be unable to keep the appointment.
```

④

```
              JOHN N. SMITH, M.D.
                   8 Main St.
               Phone 259-7328
              Ms. K. Lee
..........................................................
              has an appointment on

..........................................................
     Day          Month          Date

At ............... A.M. ............. P.M. .............
_____
Please telephone one day in advance if you
will be unable to keep the appointment.
```

⑤

```
              JOHN N. SMITH, M.D.
                   8 Main St.
               Phone 259-7328
              Mr. G. Rice
..........................................................
              has an appointment on

..........................................................
     Day          Month          Date

At ............... A.M. ............. P.M. .............
_____
Please telephone one day in advance if you
will be unable to keep the appointment.
```

⑥

```
              JOHN N. SMITH, M.D.
                   8 Main St.
               Phone 259-7328
              Ms. N. Rice
..........................................................
              has an appointment on

..........................................................
     Day          Month          Date

At ............... A.M. ............. P.M. .............
_____
Please telephone one day in advance if you
will be unable to keep the appointment.
```

E. Circle T for True or F for False.

1. The doctor is a woman.   T   F

2. The man lies down on the floor.   T   F

3. The man goes to the school.   T   F

4. The doctor sits down.   T   F

5. The man has an appointment to see Dr. Lee.   T   F

6. The doctor says, "Take off your shirt."   T   F

7. The doctor listens to his heart.   T   F

F. Fill in the blanks.

The man goes to a clinic. He has an _____ to see Dr. Lee. He

1

_____ into the room and is surprised. The doctor is a _____.

2   3

She says, "_____ down in this chair." Then the doctor says,

4

"_____ off your shirt and your pants." The man is embarrassed. He

5

doesn't want to _____ off his pants. He _____ down on

6   7

the table and she _____ to his heart.

8

G. Write the story.

Look at these words from the story.

clinic	woman	embarrassed
appointment card	sit down	lie down
doctor	take off	listen to

Work with your teacher or a partner. Write other words you remember from the story.

_____

_____

Now write the story. Use the words to help you.

Exact Change

A. Talk about the pictures. Then listen to the story.

B. Number the pictures in order. Then tell the story.

C. Match the picture with the sentence.

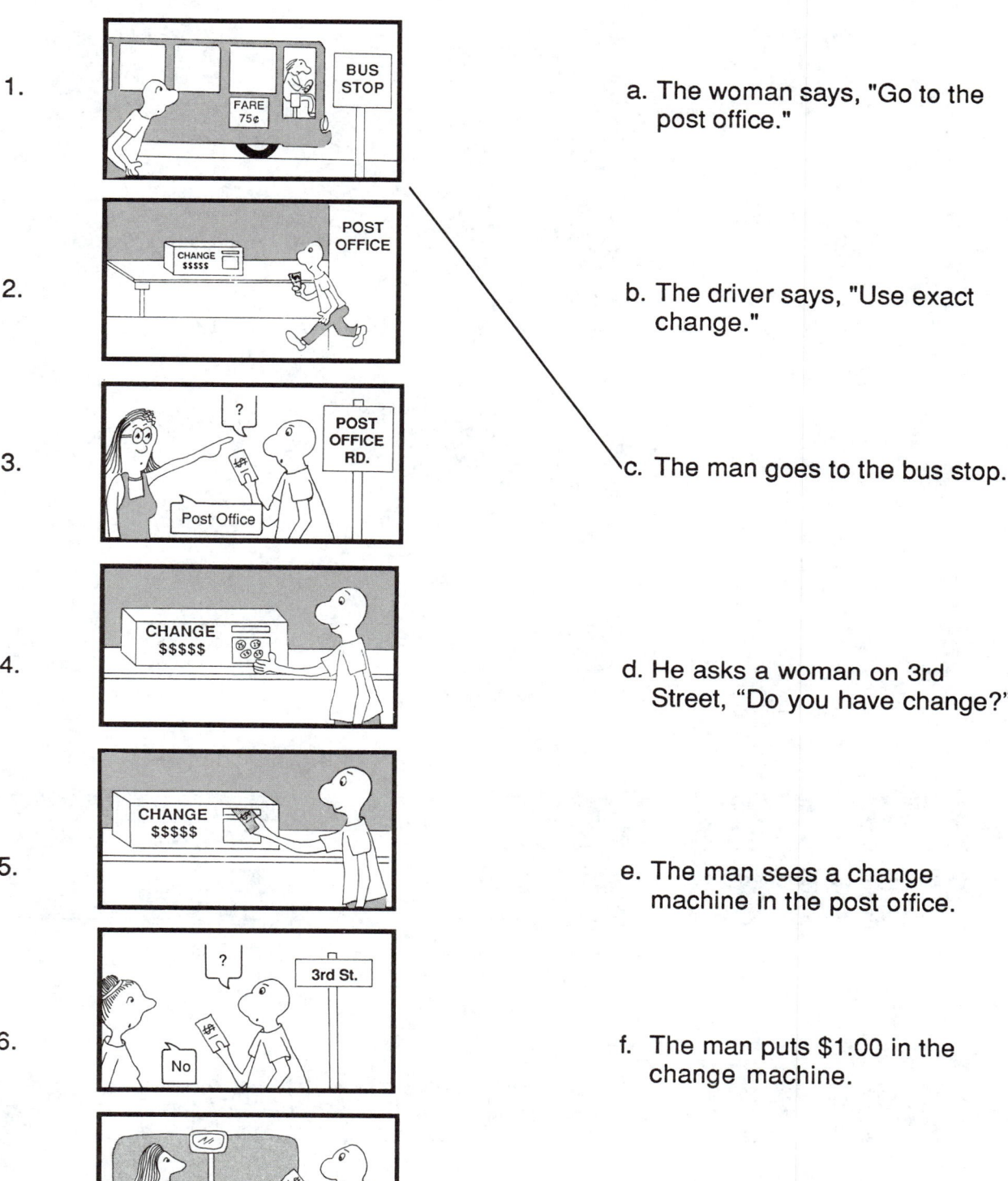

1.

a. The woman says, "Go to the post office."

2.

b. The driver says, "Use exact change."

3.

c. The man goes to the bus stop.

4.

d. He asks a woman on 3rd Street, "Do you have change?"

5.

e. The man sees a change machine in the post office.

6.

f. The man puts $1.00 in the change machine.

7.

g. The man gets 4 quarters from the change machine.

D. Listen to the teacher. Circle the correct change.

1. a.    b.    c.

2. a.    b.    c.

3. a.    b.    c.

4. a.    b.    c.

5. a.    b.   c.

6. a.    b.   c.

E. Circle T for True or F for false.

1. The man saw a change machine on 3rd St.   T   F

2. The man got off the bus with a dollar.   T   F

3. The man ran to the bus stop with his change.   T   F

4. The man asked a woman, "Do you have change?"   T   F

5. The man got on the bus with 3 quarters.   T   F

6. The bus driver said, "Put $2.00 in the fare box."   T   F

7. The man went to the post office.   T   F

F. Fill in the blanks.

A man wanted to take a bus in a large city. What happened?

1. He _____ to the bus stop.

2. He _____ on the bus.

3. The driver said, "_____ exact change in the fare box."

4. The man did not have exact change. He _____ off the bus.

5. The man asked a woman on 3rd St., "Do you have _____?"

6. A woman on Post Office Rd. said, "_____ to the post office."

7. The man _____ a change machine in the post office.

8. He _____ $1.00 in the change machine.

9. He got 4 _____.

10. He _____ to the bus stop. The bus was gone.

G. **Write the story.**
   Look at these words from the story.

bus stop	exact change	change machine
fare	get off	4 quarters
get on	post office	run

Work with your teacher or a partner. Write other words you remember from the story.

_____

_____

Now write the story. Use the words to help you.

Four-Day Job

A. Talk about the pictures. Then listen to the story.

C. Match the picture with the sentence.

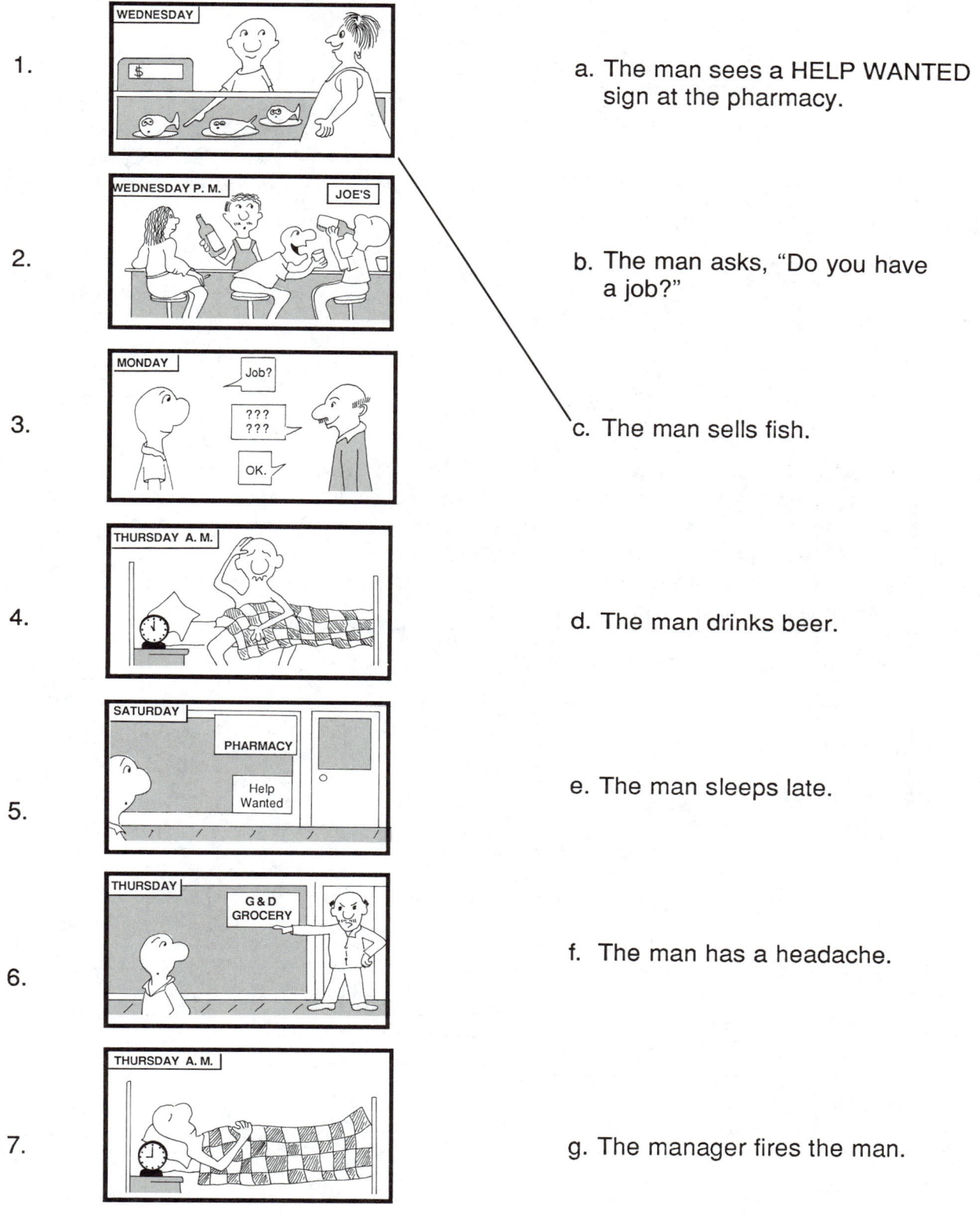

1.

2.

3.

4.

5.

6.

7.

a. The man sees a HELP WANTED sign at the pharmacy.

b. The man asks, "Do you have a job?"

c. The man sells fish.

d. The man drinks beer.

e. The man sleeps late.

f. The man has a headache.

g. The manager fires the man.

D. CROSSWORD PUZZLE. Fill in the blanks. Write the words in the crossword puzzle.

1. MONDAY, _____TUES____ DAY, WEDNESDAY

2. FRIDAY, _____ DAY, SUNDAY

3. WEDNESDAY, _____ DAY, FRIDAY

4. SATURDAY, _____ DAY, MONDAY

5. SUNDAY, _____ DAY, TUESDAY

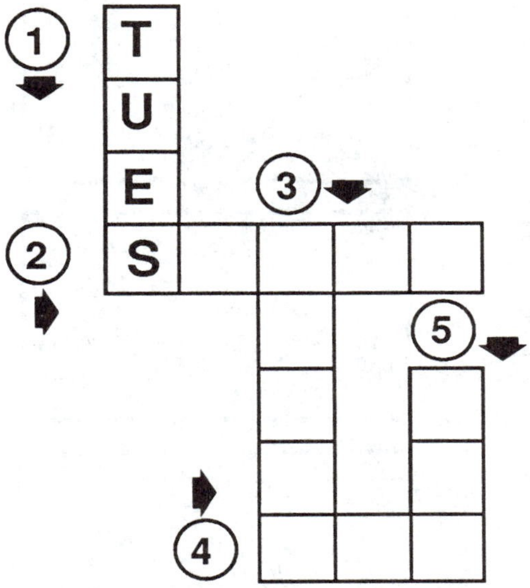

E. TIME CARD GAME. Play with a partner. One is A. One is B. Take turns. Put your marker on Start. Throw one of the dice. Move your marker. Read the name. **Player A:** Write the name. Write it in Time Card A. Move your marker to the first X. **Player B:** Write the name. Write it in Time Card B. Move your marker to the first X. Throw the dice again. Read and write the day. Move to the second X. Repeat with Time In and Time Out.

Start	Pat	Sam	John	Lee	Kate	Maria	
5:00 p.m.							Mon.
4:45 p.m.							Tues.
5:30 p.m.							Wed.
4:00 p.m.							Thurs.
4:30 p.m.							Fri.
3:45 p.m.							Sat.
	8:00 a.m.	7:45 a.m.	8:15 a.m.	8:30 a.m.	9:00 a.m.	7:00 a.m.	

TIME CARD GAME

TIME CARD A

NAME _____
DAY _____
TIME IN _____
TIME OUT _____

TIME CARD B

NAME _____
DAY _____
TIME IN _____
TIME OUT _____

F. Circle T for True or F for False.

1. The man gets a job at a grocery store.   T   F

2. The man works at a bar.   T   F

3. The manager sleeps late.   T   F

4. The manager fires the man.   T   F

5. The manager is angry.   T   F

6. The man sells fish at a pharmacy.   T   F

7. The man looks for a new job.   T   F

THURSDAY A. M.

G. Fill in the blanks.

The man is looking for a _____. He sees a Help Wanted sign. The
                                1

owner of the G and D _____ store gives him a job at the _____
                        2   3

counter on Monday. Several people come to the _____ to buy fish
                                                    4

on Tuesday. On Wednesday night he goes to a _____. He drinks
                                              5

too much beer. On Thursday, he _____ late. He arrives _____
                                  6   7

at the store. The manager is _____. He fires the man. On Friday the
                                  8

man _____ for a new job.
    9

Write the story.
Look at these words from the story.

Help Wanted	manager	drink
look for	fish	sleep late
job	bar	fire

Work with your teacher or a partner. Write other words you remember from the story.

_____

_____

Now write the story. Use the words to help you.

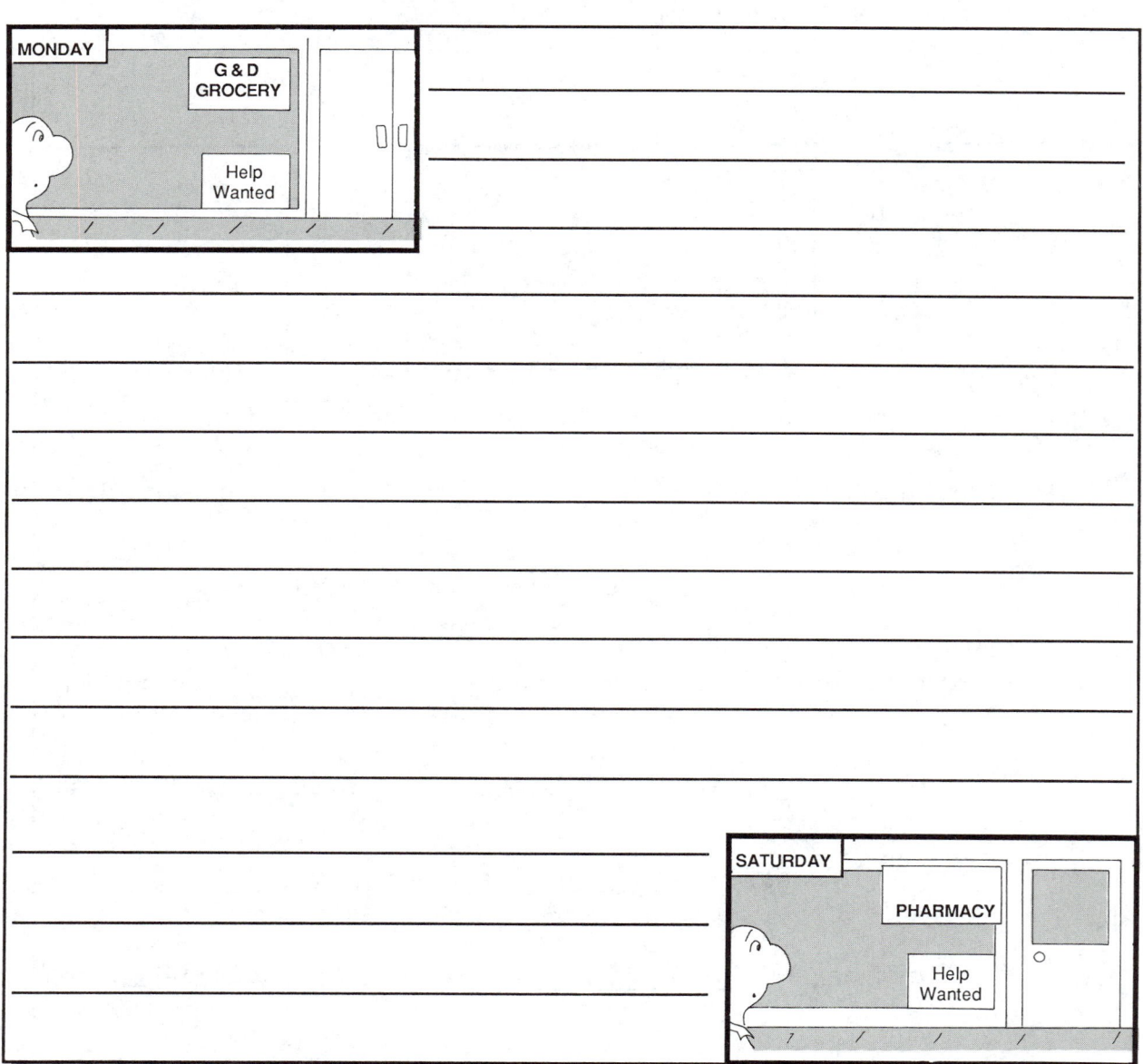

Gas

A. Talk about the pictures. Then listen to the story.

B. Number the pictures in order. Then tell the story.

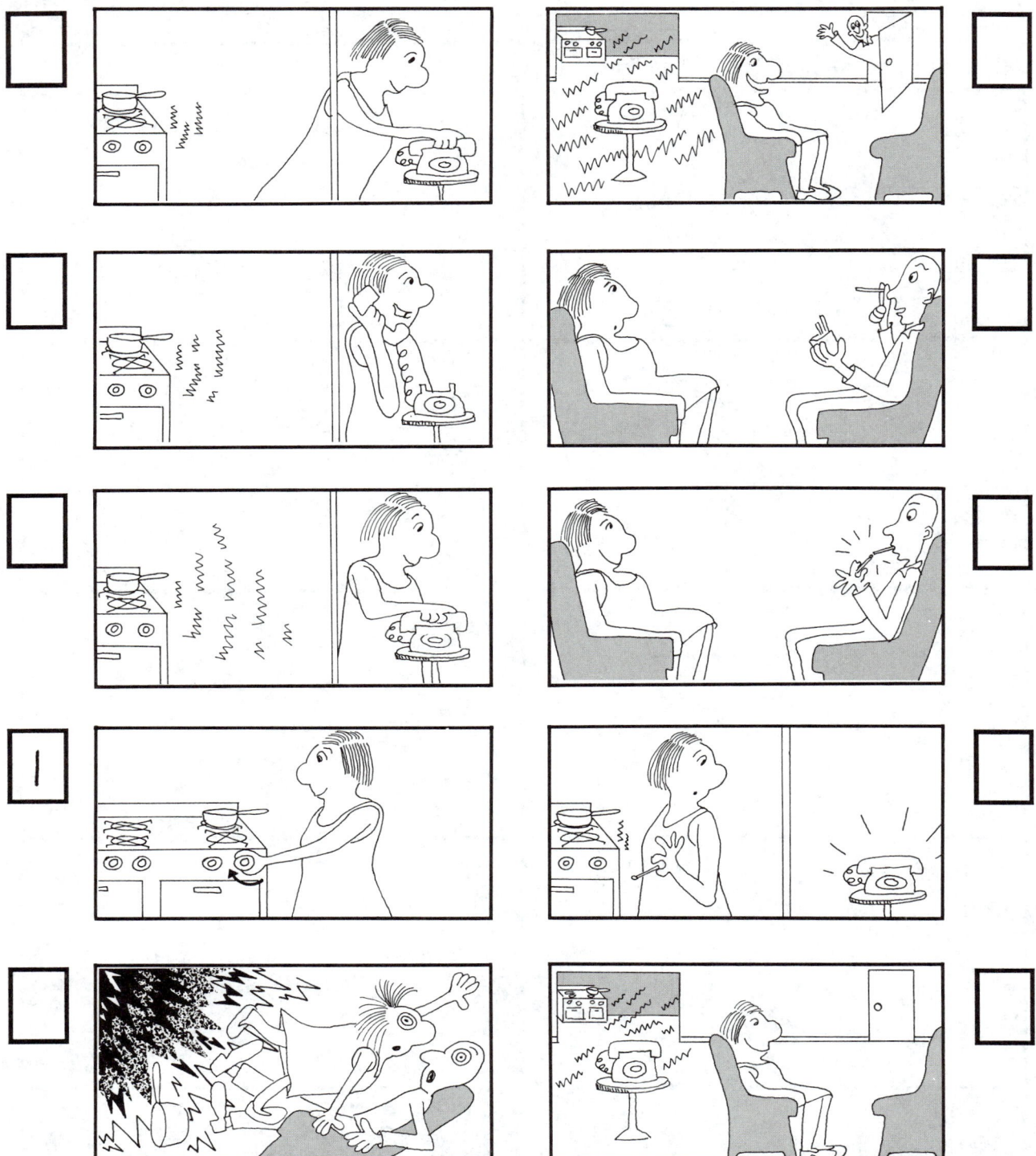

38   Unit 7

C. Match the picture with the sentence.

1.

2.

3.

4.

5.

6.

7.

a. The woman goes to answer the phone.

b. The woman talks on the phone.

c. The man lights a cigarette.

d. The woman turns on the stove.

e. The house blows up.

f. The man comes home.

g. The phone rings.

D. Look at the pictures and the words. Circle the words you don't know. Ask the meaning. Match the pictures with the words.

1.

2.

3.

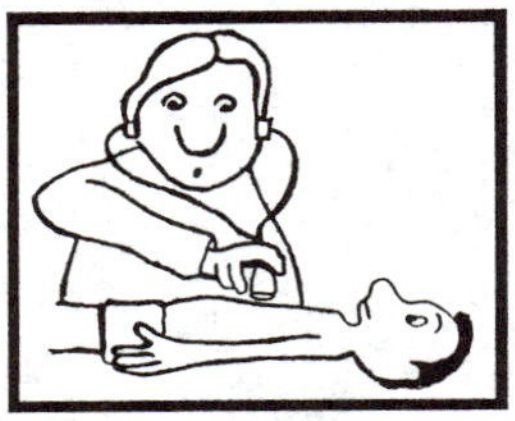

4.

5.

6.

7.

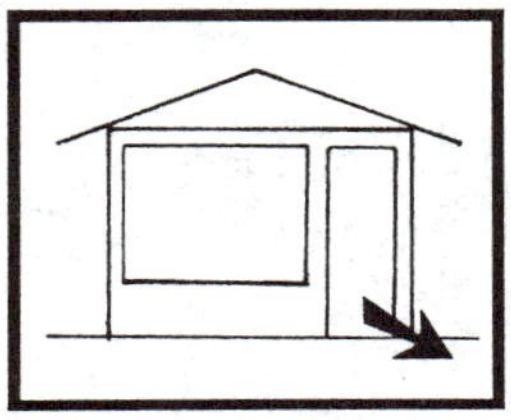

a. NO SMOKING

b. DANGER

c. POISON

d. POLICE

e. EXIT

f. DOCTOR

g. EMERGENCY

E. CROSSWORD PUZZLE. Write the words for picture 1 in the spaces after the number 1. Continue in the same way with the other numbers.

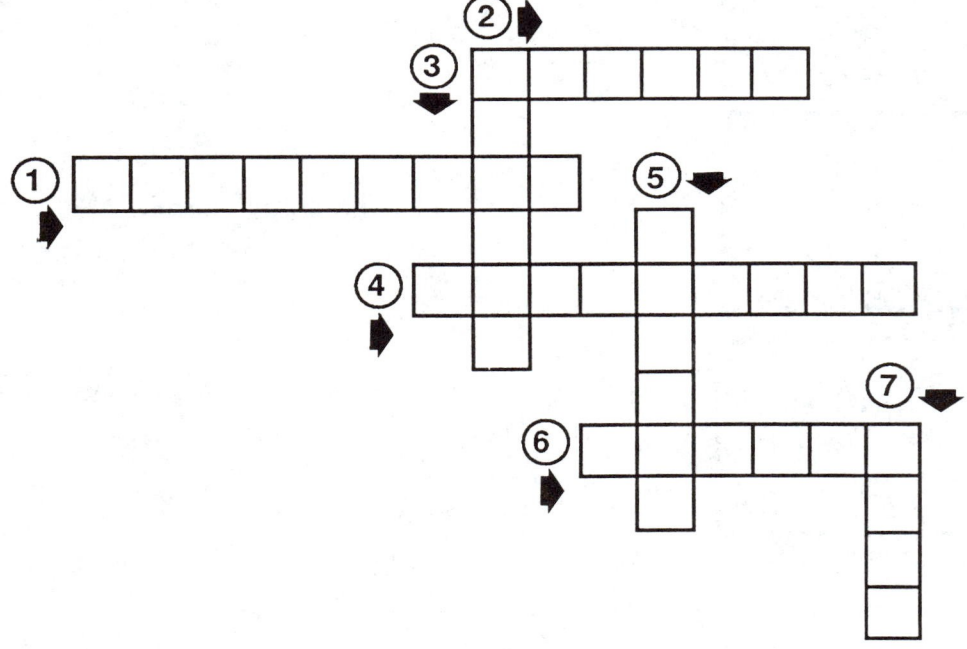

F. Circle T for True or F for False.

1. The woman lights a cigarette.   T   F

2. The house blows up.   T   F

3. The phone rings.   T   F

4. The woman turns off the gas stove.   T   F

5. The woman and man sit down in the kitchen.   T   F

6. The woman hangs up a picture.   T   F

7. The man comes home.   T   F

G. Fill in the blanks.

A woman turns on the gas stove. The phone _____ and she
                                                    1

_____ it. She forgets to _____ off the gas stove.
        2   3

She _____ up the phone and _____ down in the living
          4   5

room. The man _____ home and sits down. He lights a
                      6

_____. The house _____ up.
        7   8

H. **Write the story.**
Look at these words from the story.

turn on	talk	come home
ring	hang up	cigarette
pick up	sit down	blow up

Work with your teacher or a partner. Write other words you remember from the story.

_____

_____

Now write the story. Use the words to help you.

A. Talk about the pictures. Then listen to the story.

C. Match the picture with the sentence.

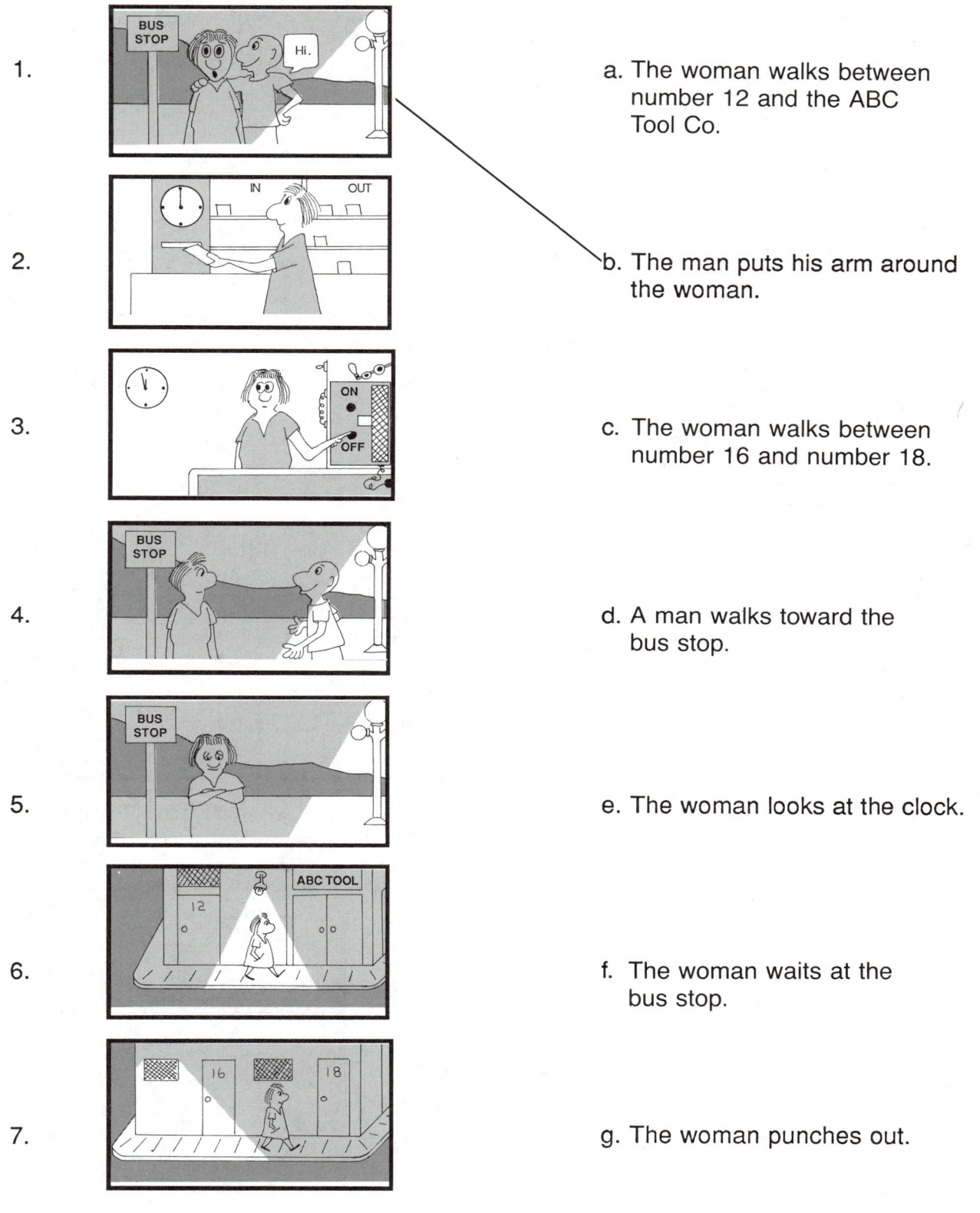

1.

a. The woman walks between number 12 and the ABC Tool Co.

2.

b. The man puts his arm around the woman.

3.

c. The woman walks between number 16 and number 18.

4.

d. A man walks toward the bus stop.

5.

e. The woman looks at the clock.

6.

f. The woman waits at the bus stop.

7.

g. The woman punches out.

D. Look at the pictures and the words. Circle the words you don't know. Ask the meaning. Match the pictures with the words.

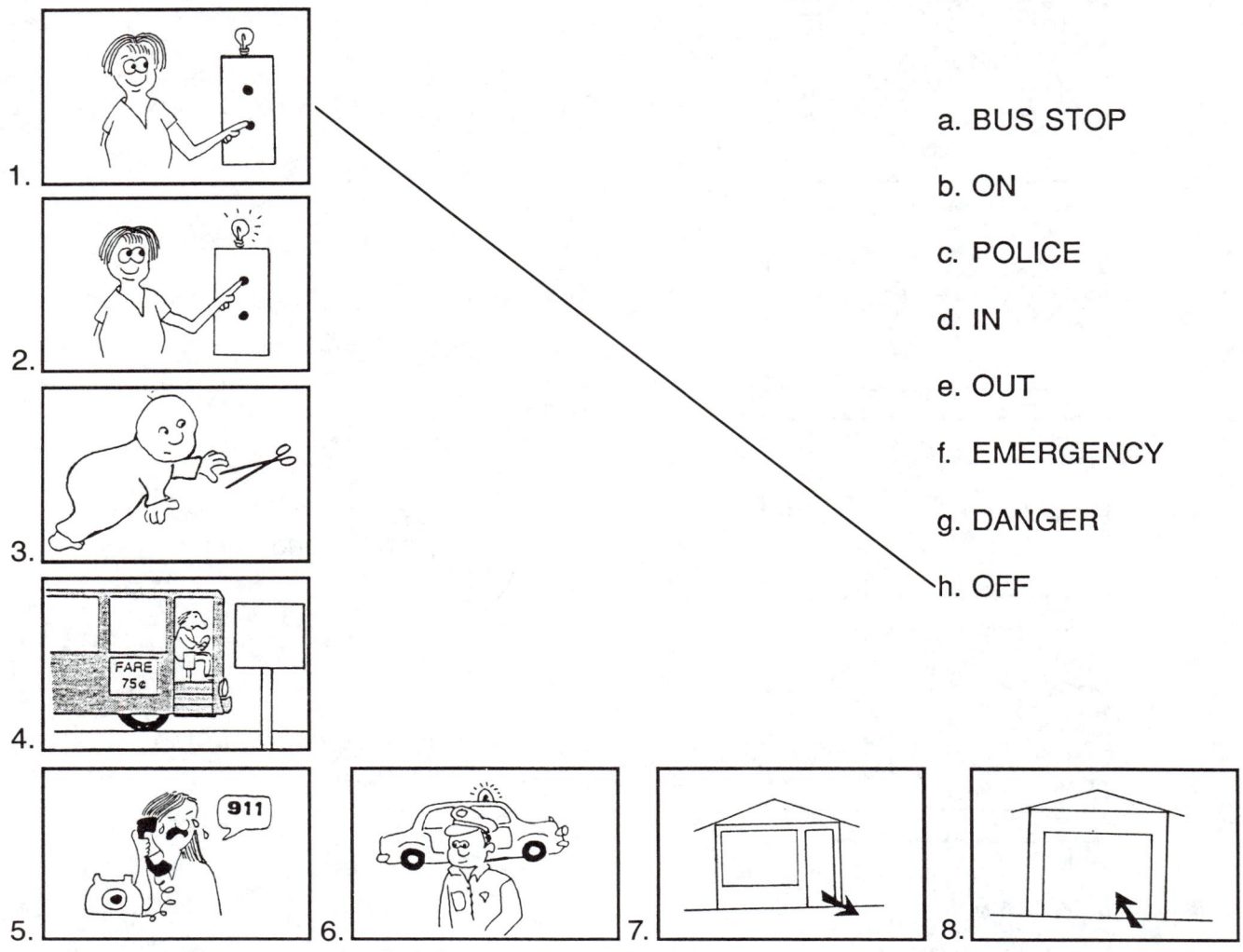

a. BUS STOP

b. ON

c. POLICE

d. IN

e. OUT

f. EMERGENCY

g. DANGER

h. OFF

E. THREE IN A ROW. Look at the words again. Write one in each box. Play with a partner. Take turns. Read a word. Put a marker on the word. The winner has 3 markers in a row.

	911	

F. Circle T for True or F for False.

1. The woman leaves work at midnight. T F

2. A man puts his arm around the woman. T F

3. The bus stop is next to the factory. T F

4. The woman works in a factory. T F

5. The woman waits at the bus stop. T F

6. The woman turns off the machine. T F

7. The woman walks with two friends. T F

G. Fill in the blanks.

A woman _____ in a factory. She leaves work at _____.
                    1   2

She _____ off the machine and punches out. She _____
      3   4

several blocks to the _____ stop. It's dark. She _____
                           5   6

at the bus stop. A _____ walks toward her. He puts his _____
                 7   8

around her. He says, "Hi."

H. Write the story.
Look at these words from the story.

midnight	walk	wait
turn off	block	arm
punch out	bus stop	

Work with your teacher or a partner. Write other words you remember from the story.

_____

_____

Now write the story. Use the words to help you.

UNIT 9 — The Neighbor's Kitchen

A. Talk about the pictures. Then listen to the story.

B. Number the pictures in order. Then tell the story.

C. Match the picture with the word. Match the word with the sentence.

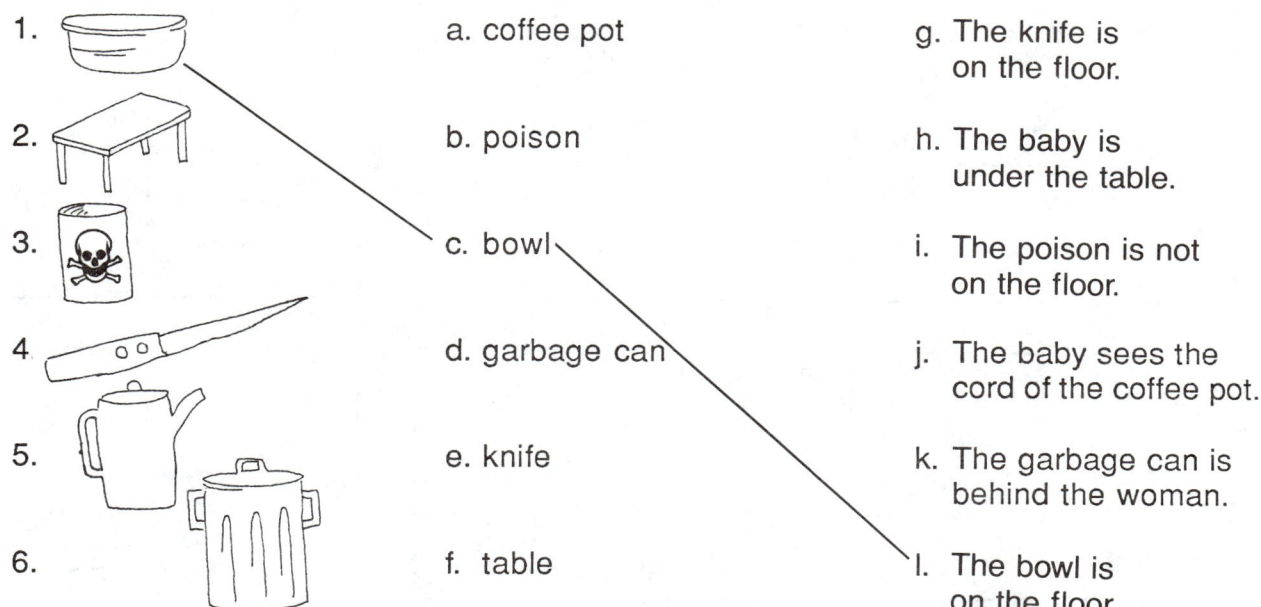

1.   a. coffee pot   g. The knife is on the floor.

2.   b. poison   h. The baby is under the table.

3.   c. bowl   i. The poison is not on the floor.

4.   d. garbage can   j. The baby sees the cord of the coffee pot.

5.   e. knife   k. The garbage can is behind the woman.

6.   f. table   l. The bowl is on the floor.

D. What is wrong in the neighbor's kitchen? Circle the problems.

E. Where's the poison? Listen to the teacher. Write the number in the box.

F. Where's the knife? Listen to the teacher. Write the number in the box.

G. Circle T for True or F for False.

1. The baby is under the table.	T	F
2. There's water on the kitchen table.	T	F
3. The woman is drinking coffee with three neighbors.	T	F
4. The poison is next to the stove.	T	F
5. The women are in the kitchen.	T	F
6. The garbage can is behind the woman.	T	F
7. The curtains are over the sink.	T	F

H. Fill in the blanks.

The woman goes to visit her neighbor.
Look at the picture in Exercise D. What does she see?

1. The spoon is _____ the bowl.
   1

2. The knife is _____ the floor.
   2

3. The curtains are _____ the stove.
   3

4. The garbage can is _____ the woman.
   4

5. The lid is _____ the garbage can.
   5

6. The poison is _____ the stove.
   6

7. Oh no! Look out! The coffee pot is _____ the table.
   Where's the baby?   7

8. The baby is _____ the table.
   8

I. Write the story.
Look at these words from the story.

neighbor	poison	water
kitchen	knife	baby
coffee	garbage	

Work with your teacher or a partner. Write other words you remember from the story.

_____

_____

Now write the story. Use the words to help you.

Numbers

A. Talk about the pictures. Then listen to the story.

B. Number the pictures in order. Then tell the story.

FIRST

SECOND

C. Match the picture with the sentence. Circle the correct number in each sentence.

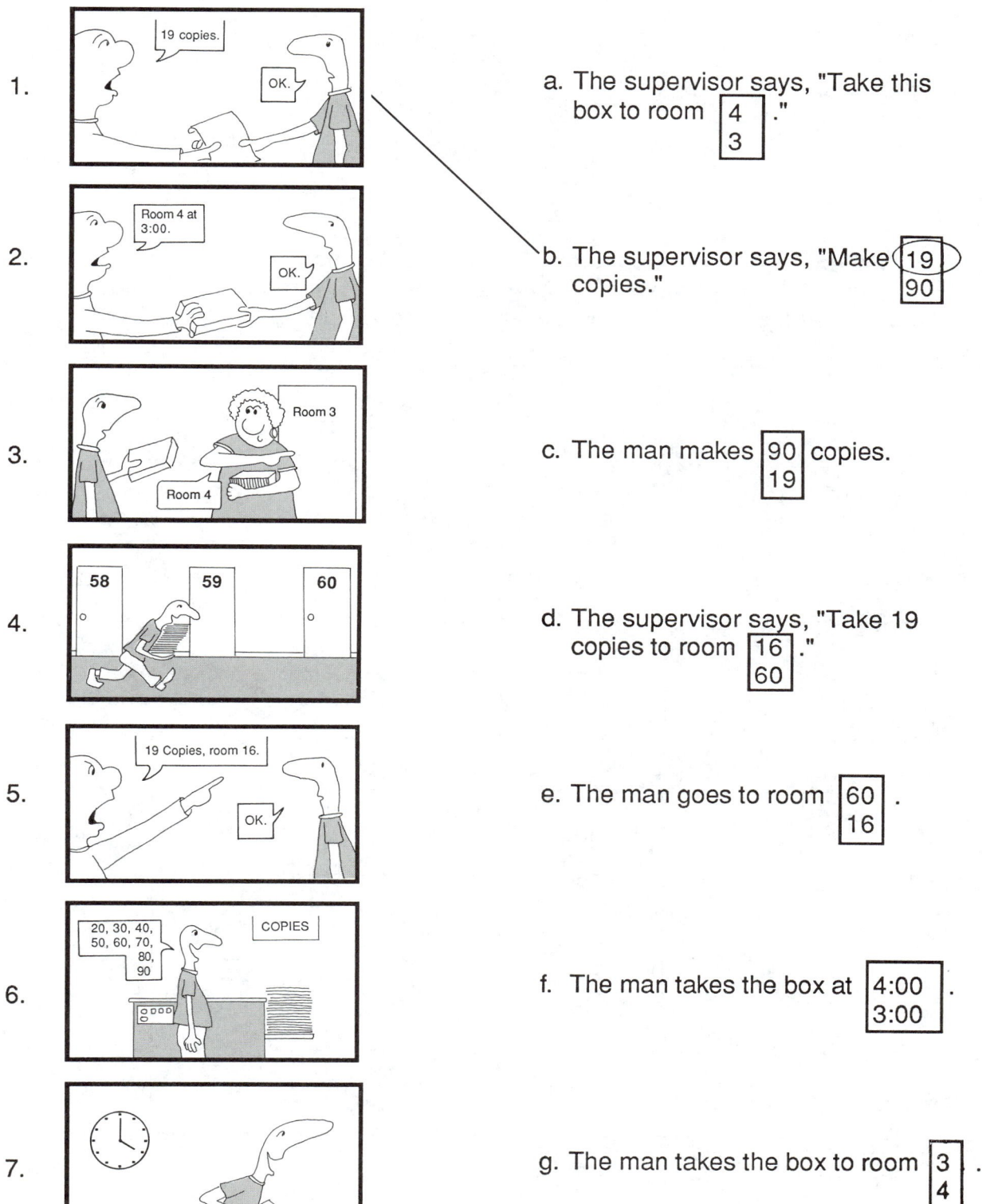

D.   Listen to the teacher. Circle the number you hear.

1. a. 19	b. 90	6. a. 14	b. 40
2. a. 80	b. 18	7. a. 8	b. 80
3. a. 30	b. 13	8. a. 50	b. 15
4. a. 16	b. 60	9. a. 9	b. 90
5. a. 70	b. 17	10. a. 7	b. 70

E. LADDER GAME. Play with a partner. Take turns. Put your marker on ENTER. Throw the dice. Move your marker. Read the number. When you land on a box with an arrow, follow the arrow. The winner gets to the EXIT first.

12:00	5	2	9:30	100	**EXIT**
22	3:00	1	0	12	70
5	77	55	5:00	33	3
40	8	3:30	10	4	6:00
6:30	66	11:30	11	19	59
7	15	4:00	6	1:30	50
7:00	16	11:00	44	80	66
30	17	99	4:30	18	9:00
ENTER	9	10:00	60	88	14

F. Circle T for True or F for False.

1. The supervisor is not angry.   T   F

2. The man makes 19 copies.   T   F

3. The man takes the copies to room 60.   T   F

4. The man goes to room 3 at 4:00.   T   F

5. The man takes a box to room 3.   T   F

6. The man in room 4 is angry.   T   F

7. The supervisor tells the man to make 19 copies.   T   F

G. Fill in the blanks.

A supervisor says to a man, "Take this box to room 4 at 3:00." The man takes the

box to _____ 3 at 4:00. The man in room 4 is angry. Then the
        1

_____ says, "Make _____ copies." The man goes to the
   2   3

copy machine. He makes 90 _____. His supervisor is _____.
                 4   5

He says, " _____ 19 copies. _____ them to room 16."
          6   7

The man takes the copies to room _____.
                       8

H. Write the story.
   Look at these words from the story.

supervisor	room	make copies
box	copy machine	angry

Work with your teacher or a partner. Write other words you remember from the story.

_____

_____

Now write the story. Use the words to help you.

UNIT 11

One Day's Work

A. Talk about the pictures. Then listen to the story.

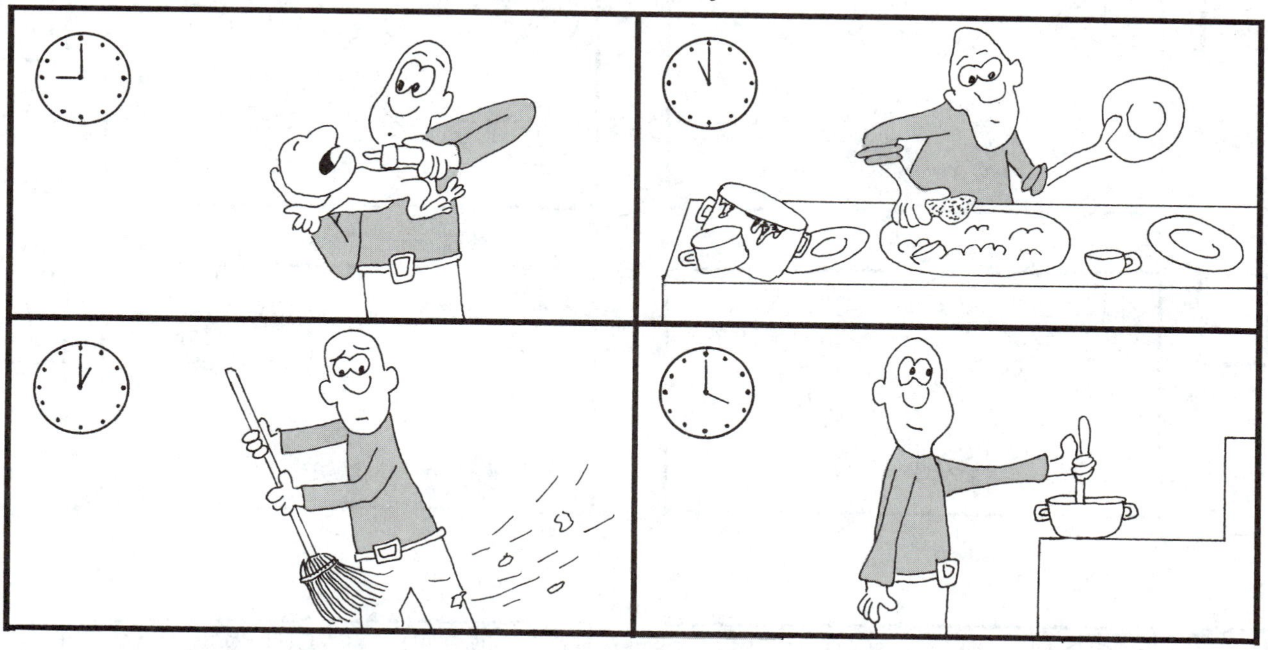

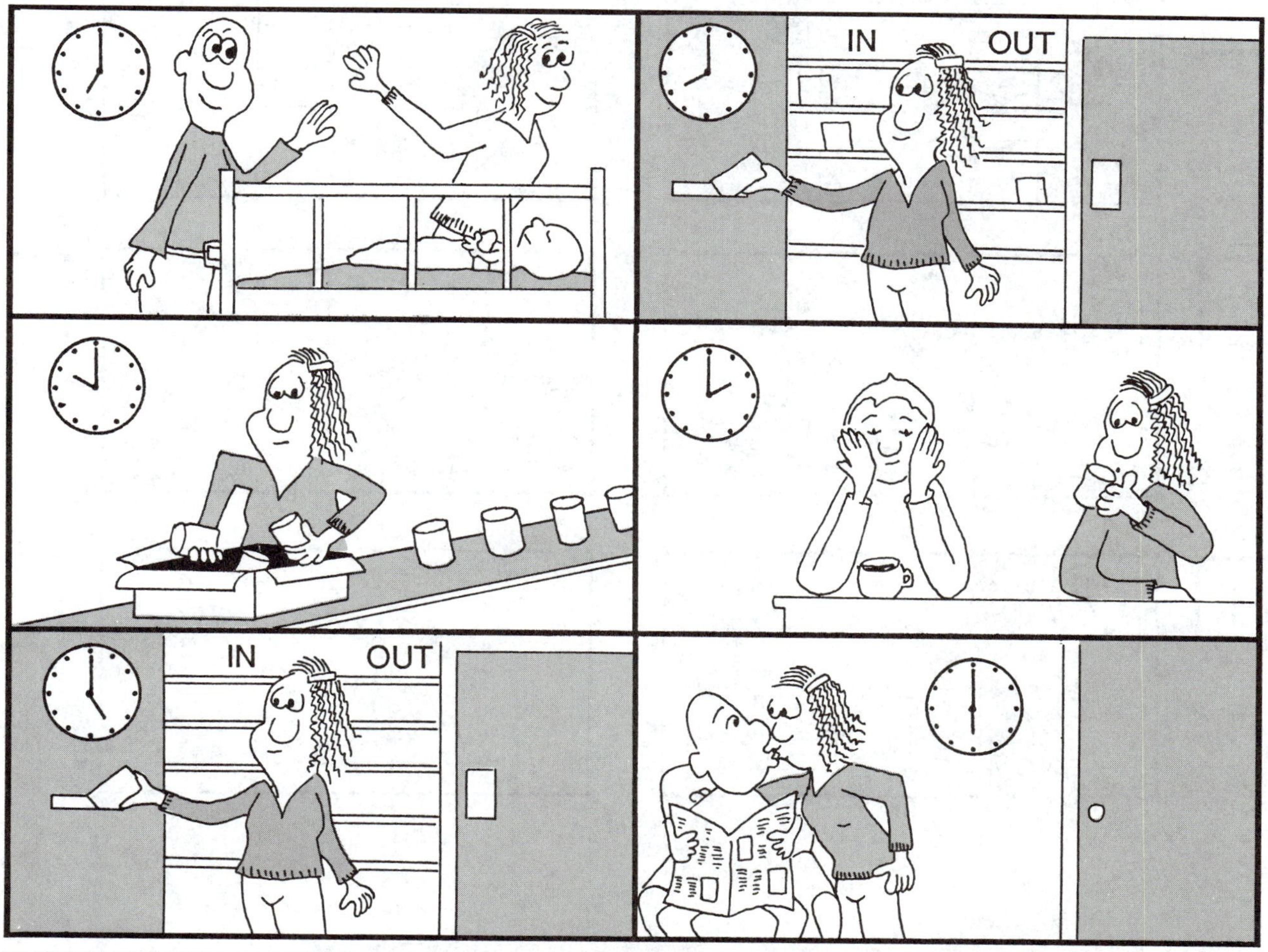

B. Number the pictures in order. Then tell the story.

FIRST

SECOND

C. Match the picture with the time. Match the time with the sentence.

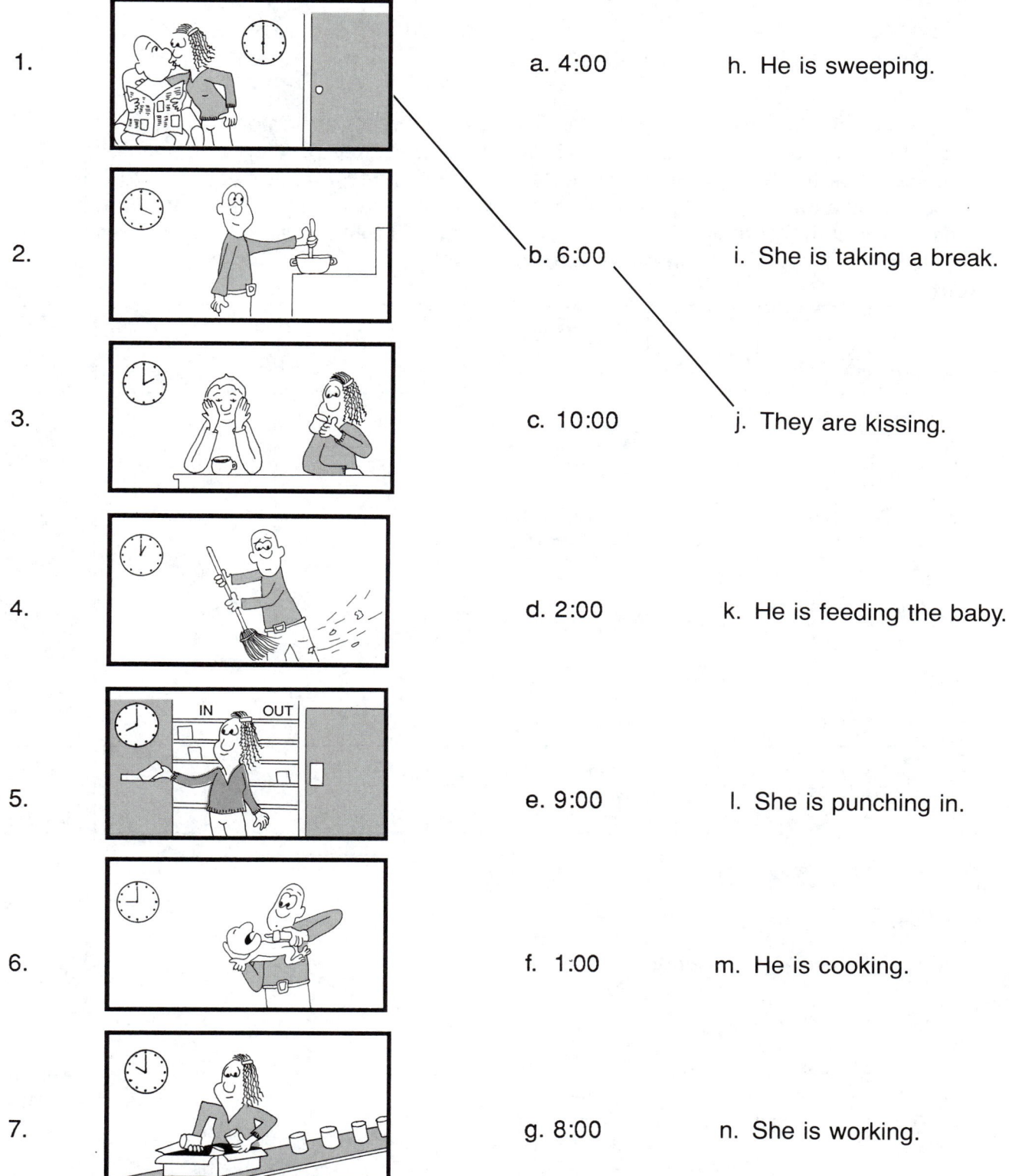

1.

a. 4:00   h. He is sweeping.

2.

b. 6:00   i. She is taking a break.

3.

c. 10:00   j. They are kissing.

4.

d. 2:00   k. He is feeding the baby.

5.

e. 9:00   l. She is punching in.

6.

f. 1:00   m. He is cooking.

7.

g. 8:00   n. She is working.

D. Look at these words. Circle the words you don't know. Ask the meaning.

cook	wash the dishes	punch in	go home
sweep	feed the baby	punch out	take a break
work	read the paper		

E. WORK GAME. Play with a partner. One is A. A works at home. One is B. B works in a factory. Take turns. Throw one of the dice. Move your marker. Look at the picture. What does this person do? **Player A:** Look at the words in Box A. Is it there? Yes: Put an X. No: Player B throws one of the dice. **Player B:** Look at the words in Box B. Is it there? Yes: Put an X. No: Player A throws one of the dice. The winner has the most X's.

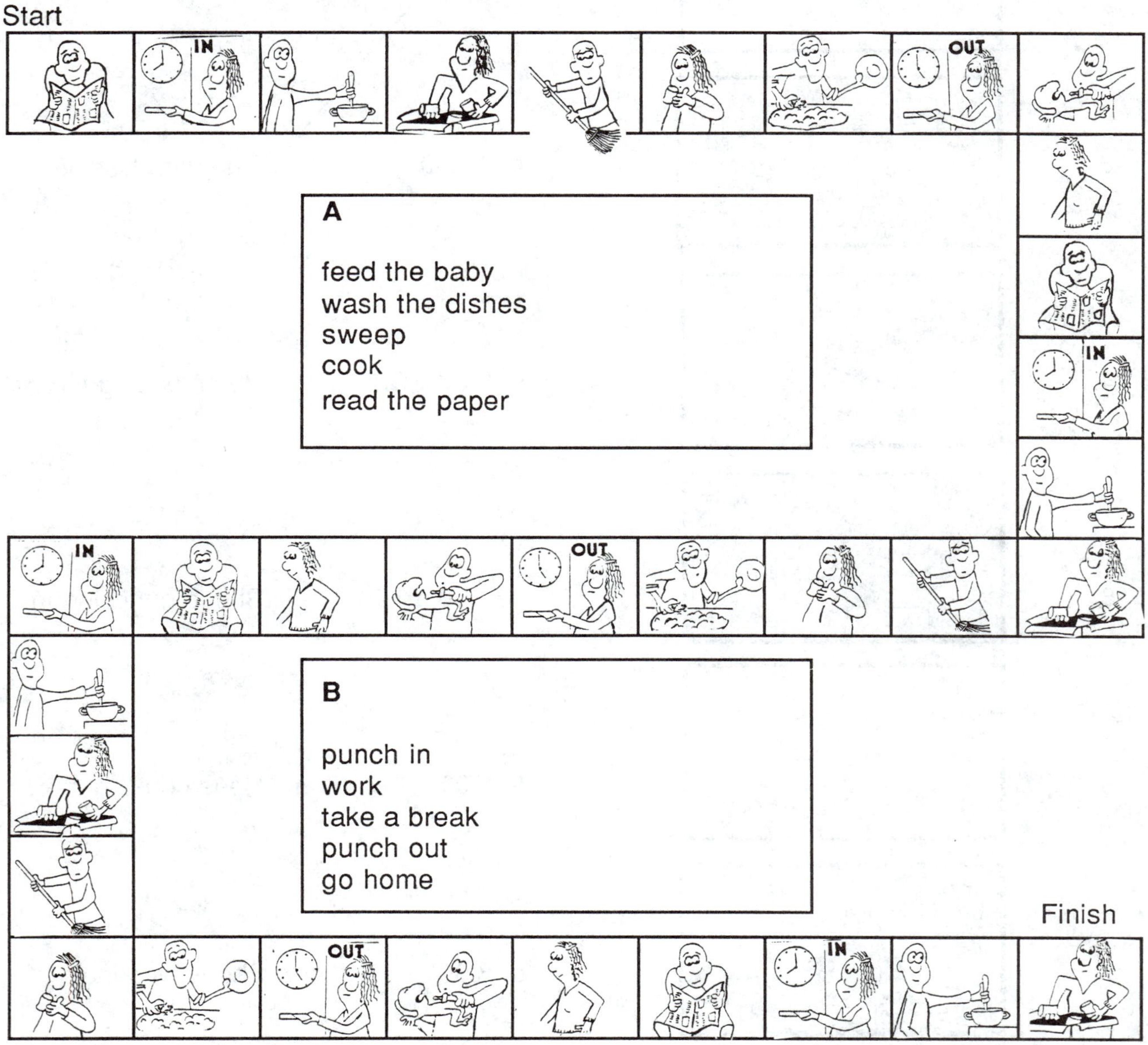

Start

A

feed the baby
wash the dishes
sweep
cook
read the paper

B

punch in
work
take a break
punch out
go home

Finish

Note: A player can put more than one X next to each word. Players only go around once. A player who reaches the finish box waits for the other player to complete the game.

F. Circle T for True or F for False.

1. The man works in a factory.   T   F

2. The woman comes home at 6:00.   T   F

3. The woman kisses her mother.   T   F

4. The man feeds two babies.   T   F

5. The woman washes the dishes and sweeps the floor.   T   F

6. The man cooks dinner.   T   F

7. The man reads a newspaper.   T   F

G. Fill in the blanks.

A man works in the home. His wife _____ in a factory. Every
                                         1

morning at 9:00, the man _____ the baby. Then he _____
                            2   3

the dishes, _____ the floor and _____ dinner. At 6:00, he
                   4   5

_____ the newspaper. His _____ arrives at work at 8:00.
   6   7

She works in a _____ from 8:00 to 5:00. At 6:00 she _____
                8   9

home and _____ her husband.
       10

H. Write the story.
Look at these words from the story.

man	woman	work
home	factory	kiss

Work with your teacher or a partner. Write other words you remember from the story.

_____

_____

Now write the story. Use the words to help you.

Pay Phone

A. Talk about the pictures. Then listen to the story.

B. Number the pictures in order. Then tell the story.

C. Match the picture with the sentence.

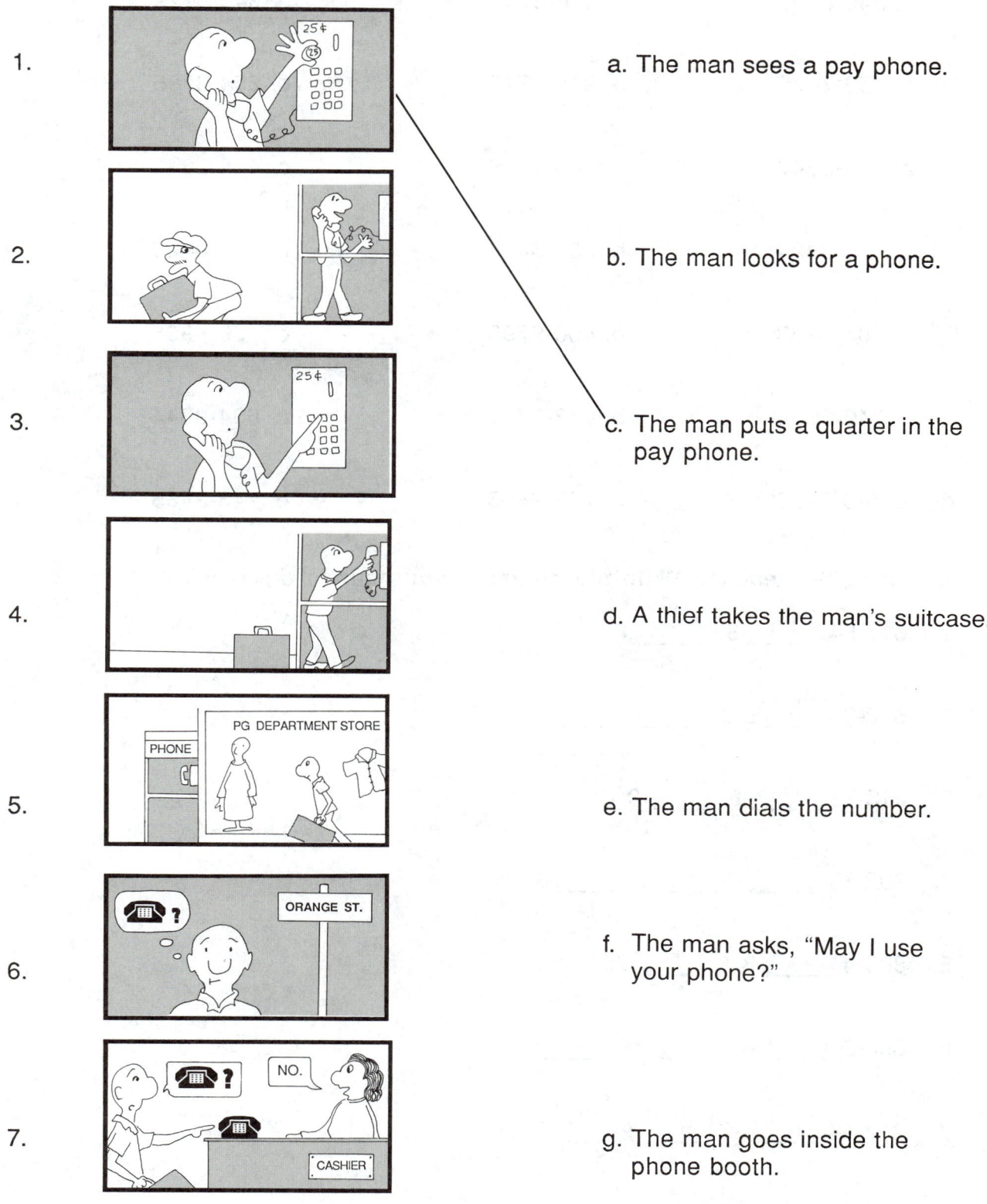

1.

2.

3.

4.

5.

6.

7.

a. The man sees a pay phone.

b. The man looks for a phone.

c. The man puts a quarter in the pay phone.

d. A thief takes the man's suitcase.

e. The man dials the number.

f. The man asks, "May I use your phone?"

g. The man goes inside the phone booth.

D. Listen to the teacher. Circle the number you hear.

1. a. 345-6798　　　　b. 346-6798　　　　c. 346-6779

2. a. 256-7685　　　　b. 245-6785　　　　c. 254-6785

3. a. 443-5847　　　　b. 443-5578　　　　c. 445-5846

4. a. 563-3424　　　　b. 564-3426　　　　c. 363-3425

5. a. 465-6923　　　　b. 456-6798　　　　c. 466-6998

6. a. 642-2354　　　　b. 643-2345　　　　c. 634-2344

7. a. 743-2456　　　　b. 743-2435　　　　c. 743-2465

E. Listen to the teacher. Write the numbers you hear in the blanks.

1. 617-54 _____-87 _____1

2. 512-3 _____ 5-6 _____ 1 _____

3. 413-77 _____-8 _____ 9 _____

4. 202-23 _____ - _____ 7 _____ 8

5. 800-4 _____ 3-6 _____ 79

6. 802-3 _____ 4- _____ 75 _____

7. 212-44 _____-8 _____ 9 _____

8. 415-3 _____ 4-95 _____ 2

F. Circle T for True or F for False.

1. The man uses the phone in the department store.   T   F

2. The man puts a quarter in the pay phone.   T   F

3. A thief takes the telephone.   T   F

4. The man dials the number.   T   F

5. The man leaves his suitcase outside the phone booth.   T   F

6. A man looks for a phone.   T   F

7. The man goes into the phone booth.   T   F

G. Fill in the blanks.

A man _____ for a phone. He _____ into the PG
            1   2

Department Store. He asks the cashier, "May I _____ the phone?"
                                                         3

She says, "No." He sees a _____ phone outside the department store.
                                  4

He goes into the phone _____. He leaves his _____
                                     5   6

outside the phone booth. He puts a _____ in the phone. He dials
                                               7

the _____. He talks on the phone. A _____ takes his
               8   9

suitcase.

H. **Write the story.**
Look at these words from the story.

phone	quarter	thief
pay phone	dial	take
phone booth	suitcase	

Work with your teacher or a partner. Write other words you remember from the story.

_____

_____

Now write the story. Use the words to help you.

Pickles

A. Talk about the pictures. Then listen to the story.

B. Number the pictures in order. Then tell the story.

C. Match the picture with the word.

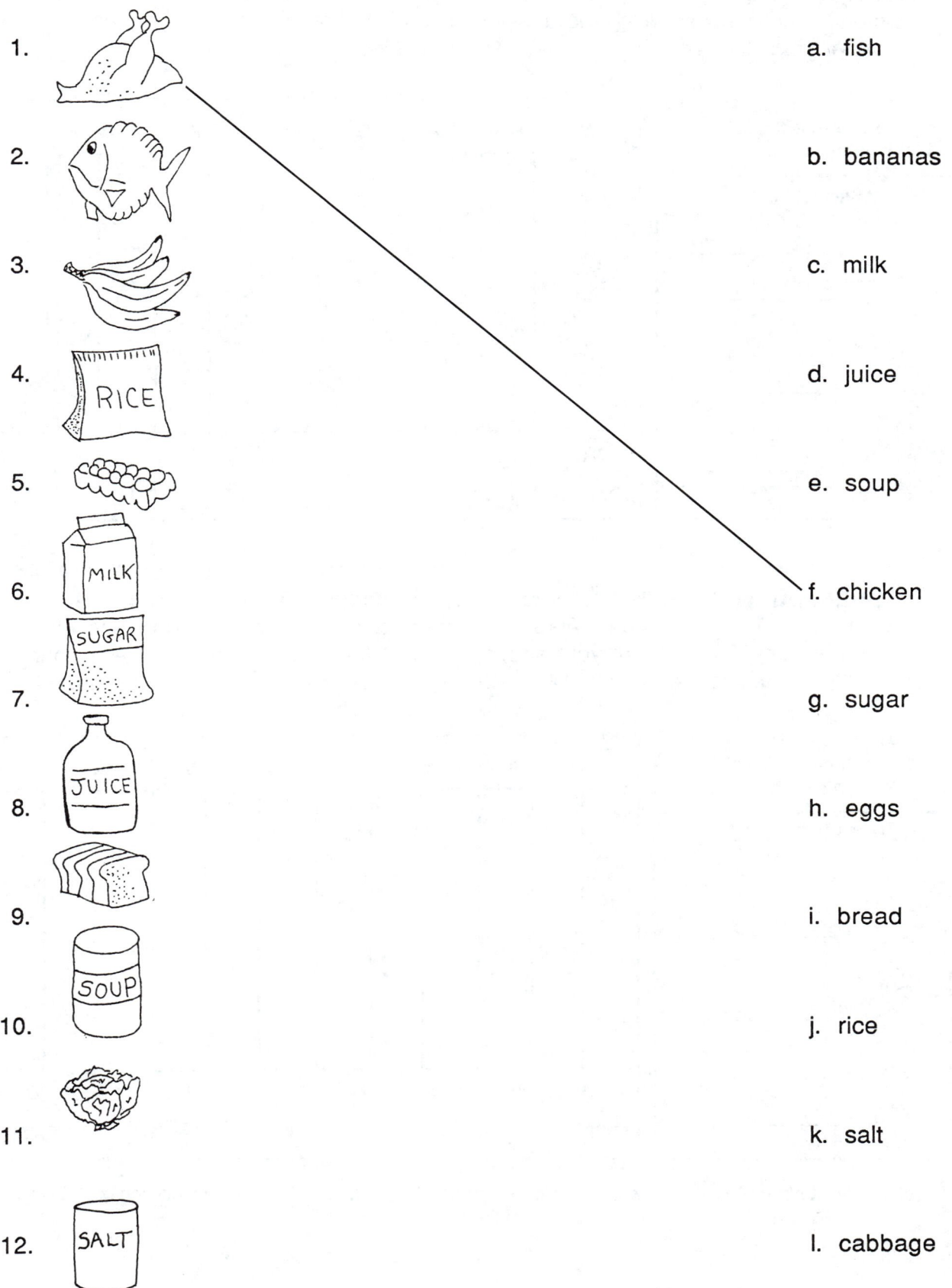

1.

2.

3.

4.   RICE

5.

6.   MILK

7.   SUGAR

8.   JUICE

9.

10. SOUP

11.

12. SALT

a. fish

b. bananas

c. milk

d. juice

e. soup

f. chicken

g. sugar

h. eggs

i. bread

j. rice

k. salt

l. cabbage

D. SUPERMARKET GAME. Play with a partner. Your partner is B. You are A.
A begins. Look at your shopping list. Where is the fish? Ask your partner.
Listen to the answer. Write the answer. Then listen to your partner's question.
Answer your partner.

A: Excuse me.
    Where is the fish?
B: In Aisle <u>3A</u>.

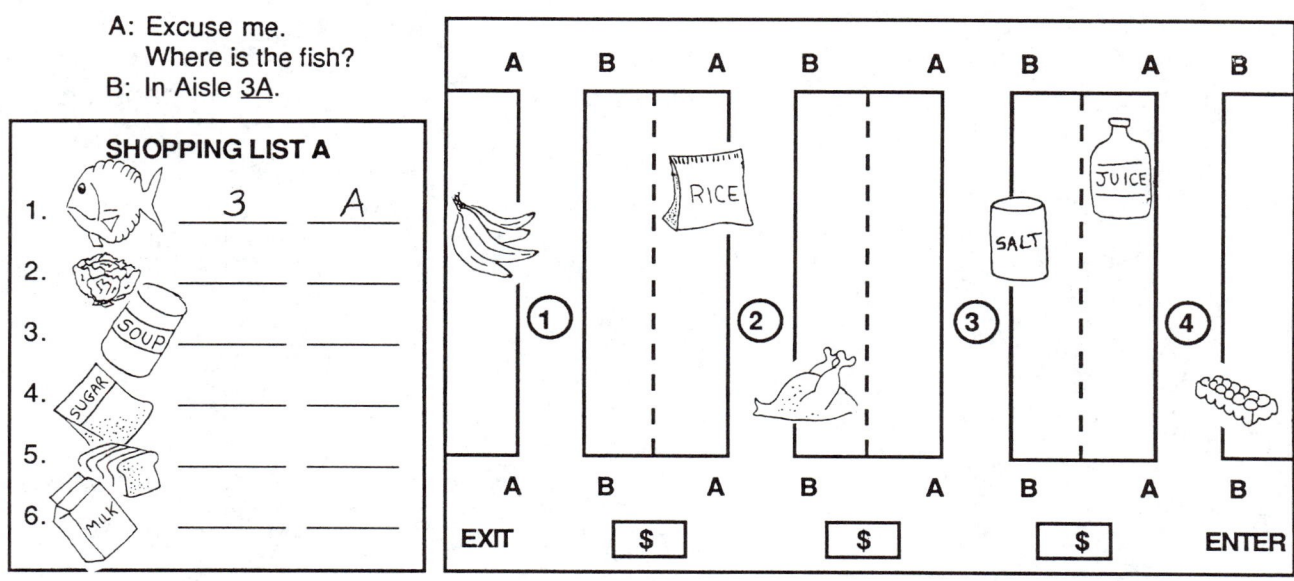

SUPERMARKET GAME. Play with a partner. Your partner is A. You are B. A
begins. Look at your supermarket. Listen to your partner's question. Answer
your partner. Then look at your shopping list. Where is the chicken? Ask your
partner. Listen to the answer. Write the answer. Continue with the other items.

A: Excuse me.
    Where is the chicken?
B: In Aisle <u>2B</u>.

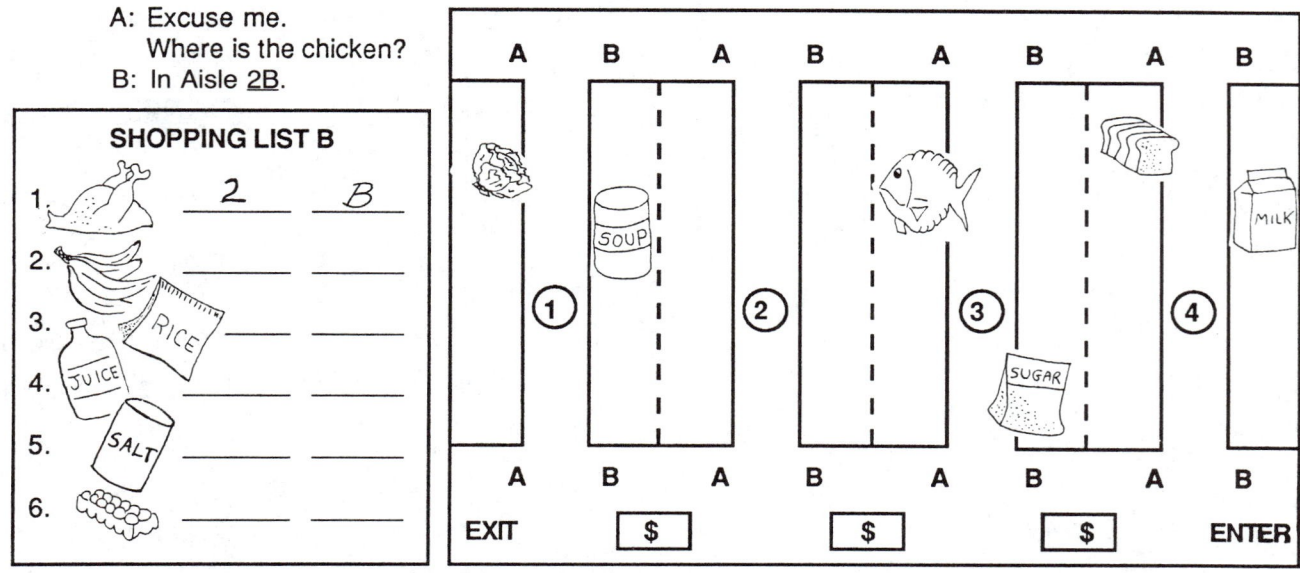

Note: Player A should cover the bottom part of this page. Player B should cover the top part of this page.

E. Circle T for True or F for False.

1. The woman went to the doctor.   T   F

2. The manager saw the woman.   T   F

3. The woman opened a bottle of milk.   T   F

4. The woman took out a banana.   T   F

5. The woman tasted a pickle.   T   F

6. The woman spit out the rice.   T   F

7. The manager said, "Pay for the pickles."   T   F

F. Fill in the blanks.

Man: Something happened in a supermarket.
Woman: What happened?

Man: A woman _____ a jar of pickles and she _____ it.
                                   1   2
Woman: She opened it?
Man: Yes, she _____ it and _____ out one pickle. Then she _____ it.
                       3   4   5
Woman: She tasted it?
Man: Yes. She _____ it and _____ it out.
                       6   7
Woman: Really? She spit it out?
Man: Yes, and the manager _____ her.
                                 8
Woman: What did he say?
Man: He said, "Pay for the _____!"
                              9

G. Write the story.
Look at these words from the story.

supermarket	take out	manager
pickles	taste	pay for
open	spit out	

Work with your teacher or a partner. Write other words you remember from the story.

_____

_____

Now write the story. Use the words to help you.

UNIT 14 The Shower

A. Talk about the pictures. Then listen to the story.

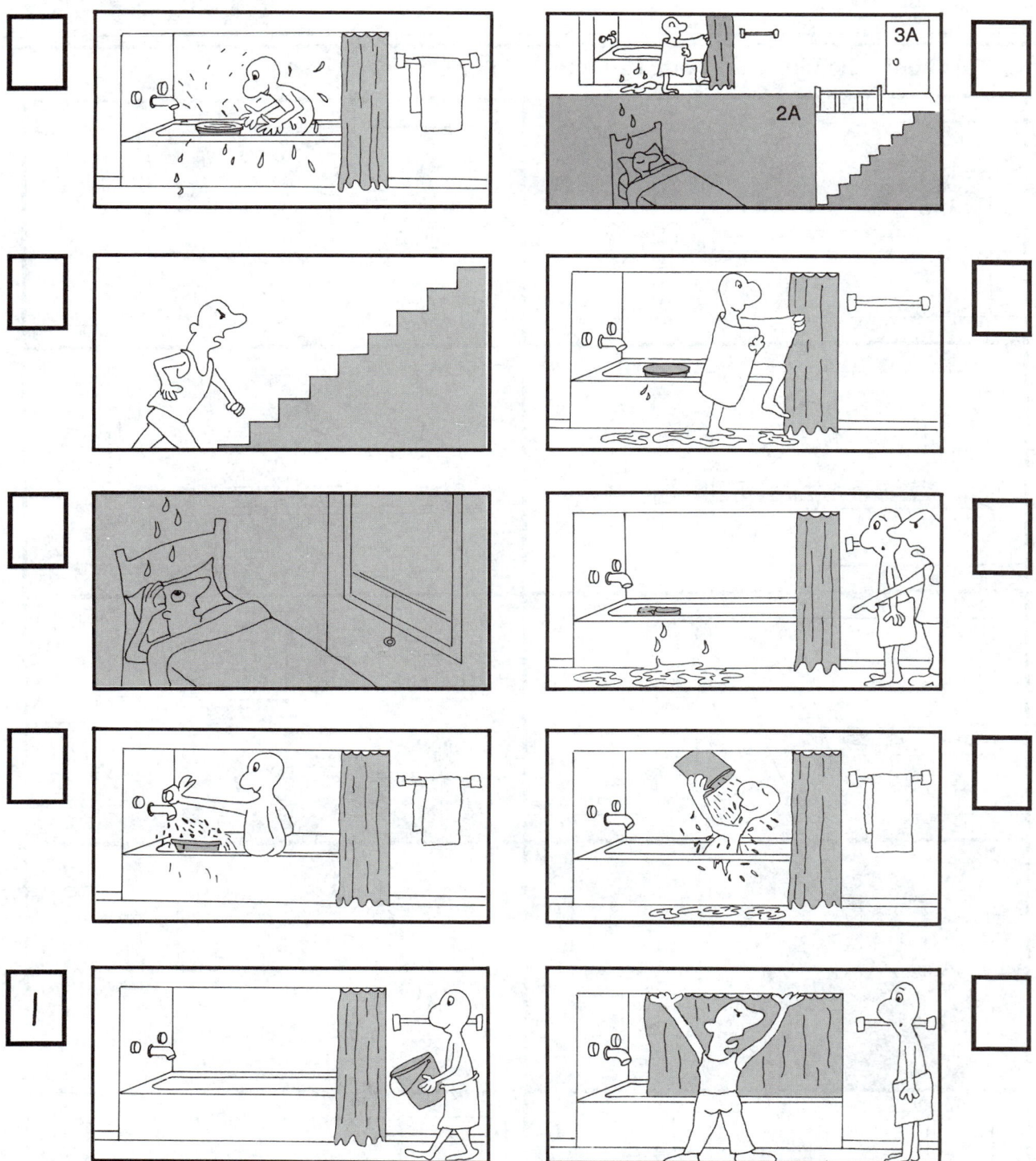

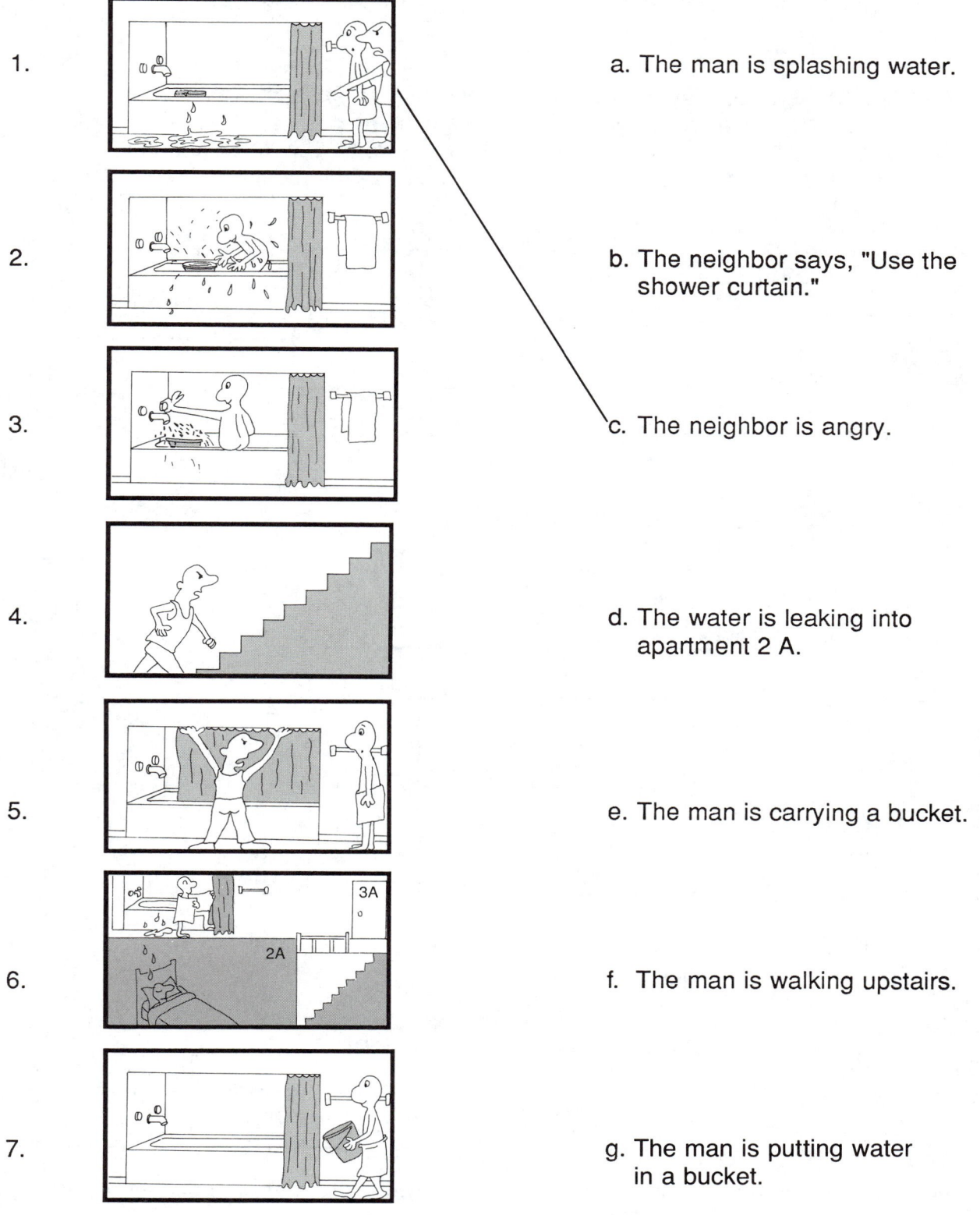

1.

2.

3.

4.

5.

6.

7.

a. The man is splashing water.

b. The neighbor says, "Use the shower curtain."

c. The neighbor is angry.

d. The water is leaking into apartment 2 A.

e. The man is carrying a bucket.

f. The man is walking upstairs.

g. The man is putting water in a bucket.

D. Look at these words. Circle the words you don't know. Ask the meaning.

bathtub	shower	shower curtain	sink
faucet	toilet	towel	

E. BATHROOM GAME. Play with a partner. One is A. One is B. Take turns. Throw one of the dice. Move your marker. Look at the picture. What is it? **Player A:** Find the word in Box A. Put an X by the word. **Player B:** Find the word in Box B. Put an X by the word. The winner has the most X's.

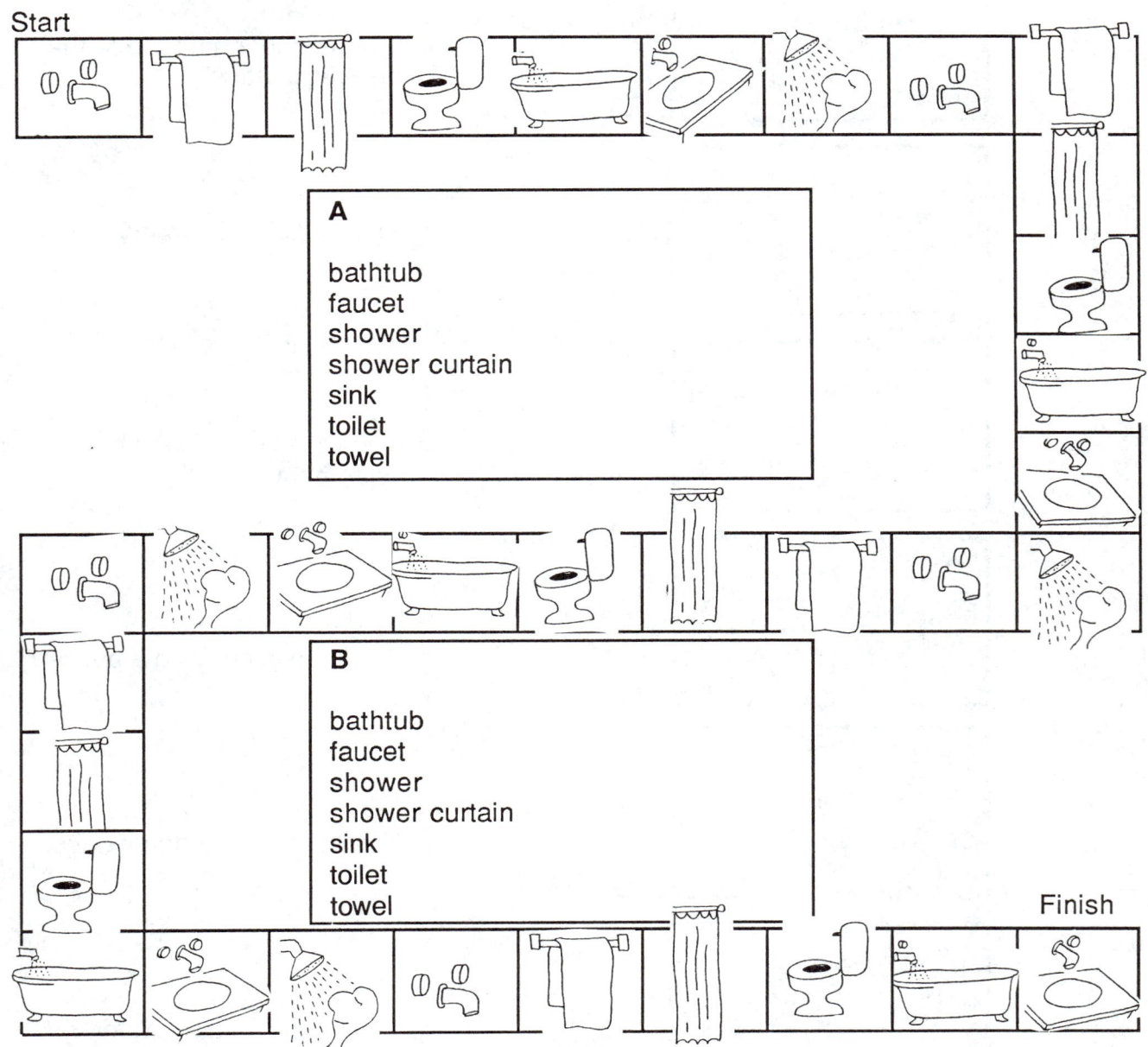

Start

A

bathtub
faucet
shower
shower curtain
sink
toilet
towel

B

bathtub
faucet
shower
shower curtain
sink
toilet
towel

Finish

Note: A player can put more than one X next to each word. Players only go around once. A player who reaches the finish box waits for the other player to complete the game.

F. Circle T for True or F for False.

1. The man is taking a shower in the kitchen.   T   F

2. The man in apartment 2A is walking upstairs.   T   F

3. The man is splashing water on the floor.   T   F

4. The man is using the shower curtain.   T   F

5. The water is leaking into his neighbor's apartment.   T   F

6. The bucket is in the bathtub.   T   F

7. The neighbor is angry.   T   F

G. Fill in the blanks.

A man is carrying a _____. He is sitting on the _____
                           1   2

and turning on the _____. He is taking a _____. He is
                       3   4

splashing water on the _____. The water is leaking into his
                               5

neighbor's _____. The man in apartment 2A is going _____.
               6   7

He is _____. He's telling the man to use the _____ curtain.
       8   9

H. Write the story.
Look at these words from the story.

bucket	leak	upstairs
water	neighbor	shower curtain
splash	angry	

Work with your teacher or a partner. Write other words you remember from the story.

_____

_____

Now write the story. Use the words to help you.

Small Fire

A. Talk about the pictures. Then listen to the story.

C. Match the picture with the sentence.

1.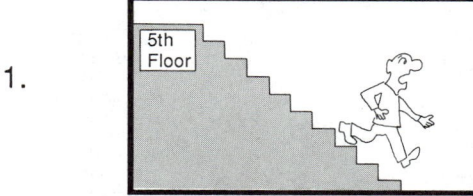
   a. He runs from the 6th floor to the 5th floor.

2.
   b. The fire is very big.

3.
   c. He tells the manager about the fire.

4.
   d. They run upstairs.

5.
   e. The man starts running.

6.
   f. A man sews clothes.

7.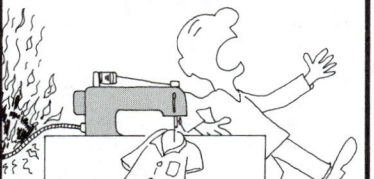
   g. He runs from the 5th floor to the 4th floor.

D. Look at the pictures and the words. Circle the words you don't know. Ask the meaning. Match the pictures with the words.

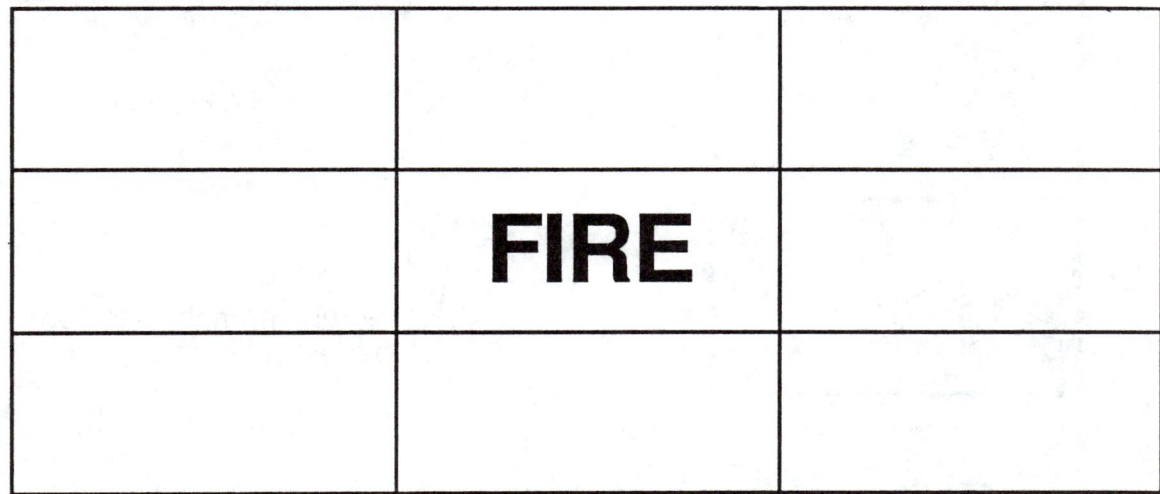

1.

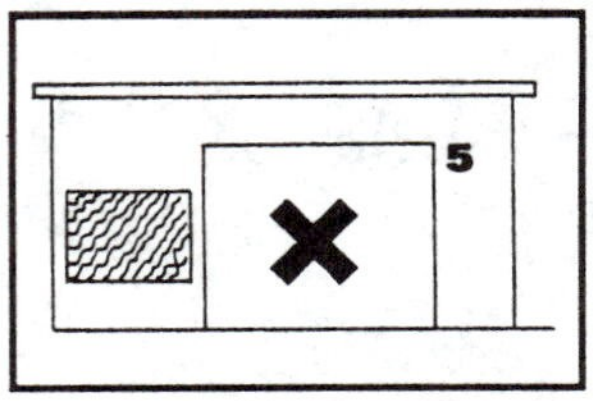

2.

3.

4.

a. EMERGENCY

b. NO SMOKING

c. DO NOT ENTER

d. POISON

e. EXIT

f. DANGER

g. ENTRANCE

h. FIRE
   EXTINGUISHER

5.   6.   7.   8.

E. THREE IN A ROW. Look at the words again. Write one in each box. Play with a partner. Take turns. Read a word. Put a marker on the word. The winner has 3 markers in a row.

	FIRE	

Note: Students should write words on the Three in a Row board in random order.

F. Circle T for True or F for False.

1. There's a fire extinguisher on the wall.   T   F

2. The man uses the fire extinguisher.   T   F

3. The manager's office is downstairs.   T   F

4. The man telephones the manager.   T   F

5. Three men run upstairs.   T   F

6. The man is afraid.   T   F

7. The man and the manager see a big fire.   T   F

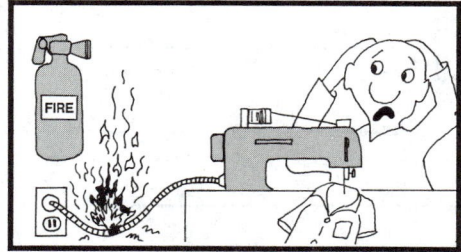

G. Fill in the blanks.

A _____ 1 _____ works in a factory. He _____ 2 _____ clothes. A small

_____ 3 _____ starts. He doesn't see the _____ 4 _____ extinguisher on

the wall. He is _____ 5 _____. He runs _____ 6 _____ to find the

manager. They _____ 7 _____ upstairs to put out the fire. They find a

_____ 8 _____ fire.

H. Write the story.
Look at these words from the story.

sew	fire extinguisher	manager
small fire	afraid	big fire

Work with your teacher or a partner. Write other words you remember from the story.

_____

_____

Now write the story. Use the words to help you.

The Wrong Message

A. Talk about the pictures. Then listen to the story.

C. Match the picture with the sentence.

1.

   a. The man waits on School Street.

2.

   b. The woman waits on Bank Street.

3.

   c. The man waits at the bank.

4.

   d. The woman says, "Tell my friend to meet me at 9:00 a.m." The man says, "OK."

5.

   e. The man says, "Go to the school on Bank St. at 9:00 p.m."

6.

   f. The woman waits at the school.

7.

   g. The woman asks, "Are you sure?" The man shouts, "Yes."

D. Listen to the teacher. Circle the place, time and day that you hear.

PLACE	TIME	DAY
1. a. Bank Street b. School Street c. 6th Street	a. 5:00 p.m. b. 4:30 p.m. c. 5:30 p.m.	a. Mon. b. Tues. c. Thurs.
2. a. 4th Street b. 7th Street c. 9th Street	a. 1:00 p.m. b. 11:00 p.m. c. 2:00 p.m.	a. Tues. b. Wed. c. Sun.
3. a. A Street b. B Street c. C Street	a. 8:15 a.m. b. 8:30 a.m. c. 8:45 a.m.	a. Sat. b. Mon. c. Tues.
4. a. L Street b. 1st Street c. D Street	a. 9:00 a.m. b. 7:00 a.m. c. 6:00 a.m.	a. Mon. b. Fri. c. Sat.
5. a. 8th Street b. 80th Street c. 9th Street	a. 11:15 p.m. b. 1:15 p.m. c. 8:15 p.m.	a. Thurs. b. Fri. c. Sun.
6. a. 9th Street b. Bank Street c. School Street	a. 9:00 a.m. b. 7:00 a.m. c. 11:00 a.m.	a. Mon. b. Tues. c. Wed.

E. MESSAGE GAME. Play with a partner. One is A. One is B. Take turns. Throw one of the dice. Move your marker. Read the name. **Player A:** Write the name. Write it in Box A. Move your marker to the first X. **Player B:** Write the name. Write it in Box B. Move your marker to the first X. Throw the dice again. Read and write the street name. Move to the second X. Repeat with days and time.

START	Tom	Sam	Maria	Lee	Jon	Pat	✕
10:00 a.m.							Bank St.
2:00 p.m.							School St.
4:00 p.m.		A			B		A St.
9:00 a.m.		NAME _____			NAME _____		1st St.
7:00 p.m.		DATE _____ DAY _____ TIME _____			DATE _____ DAY _____ TIME _____		M St.
8:00 a.m.							5th St.
✕	Sat.	Fri.	Thurs.	Wed.	Tues.	Mon.	✕

F. Circle T for True and F for False.

1. A woman wants to meet a friend.   T   F

2. The woman waits for her friend at 9:00 a.m.   T   F

3. The woman meets her friend at the bank.   T   F

4. The woman goes to the school at 9:00 p.m.   T   F

5. The man and the woman do not meet.   T   F

6. A woman gives a message to a man.   T   F

7. The man says, "Yes, I gave your friend the message."   T   F

G. Fill in the blanks.

On Monday a woman _____ a man a message for her friend. The
                                          1

man gives her friend the _____. Her friend goes to meet her at the
                                    2

_____ on School Street at 9:00 a.m. The woman _____
             3   4

to the school on Bank Street at _____ a.m. On Tuesday the _____
                                          5   6

calls the man again. She asks, "Did you give my _____ the mes-
                                                              7

sage?" The man _____, "Yes." The woman gives the message
                          8

again. The woman goes to the _____ at 9:00 a.m. The friend goes
                                          9

to the school at 9:00 _____. They are both angry.
                              10

H. Write the story.

Look at these words from the story.

message	school	a.m.
meet	bank	p.m.
wait for		

Work with your teacher or a partner. Write other words you remember from the story.

_____

_____

Now write the story. Use the words to help you.

Teacher's Notes

UNIT 1   ¹/₂ CUP

Subject

Housework, Following Directions, Measurement

Situation

Doing laundry at home. A man uses detergent from a box but reads the directions incorrectly. *Last frame:* Soap fills the basement.

Cultural Notes

In nonindustrial societies, household appliances such as washing machines are not common. When clothes are washed by hand, following written instructions on a box of soap powder precisely is not essential. Even students with basic literacy skills may have problems when directions are written using fractions and cups since they may be familiar only with the metric system.

Exercises

A Frames

1. A man takes his dirty clothes downstairs.
2. He puts the clothes in the washing machine.
3. He picks up a box of soap.
4. He looks at the directions on the box. He reads, "Use ¹/₂ cup."
5. He pours soap into a cup.
6. He pours the soap into the washing machine. He says "1 cup."
7. He pours more soap into the cup.
8. He pours the soap into the washing machine. He says, "2 cups."
9. He goes upstairs.
10. He sits down and reads a newspaper. There's a lot of soap.

B Sequencing

Answers: First column: 7(5), 3, 2, 4, 1. Second column: 10, 5(7), 6, 8, 9.

C Matching

Answers: 1. c   2. a   3. d   4. e   5. b

D Matching

Teach the concept of one cup, using a measuring cup to show markings for 1 cup and ¹/₂ cup.
Answers: 1. b   2. d   3. e   4. a   5. c

E Game Vocabulary

Teach concepts by bringing in a measuring cup, a box of detergent with written directions, a bottle of bleach, and a picture of a washing machine.

F Game

Have students play the game. (See Introduction, Play the Game, page v.)

G True/False

Answers: 1. F   2. F   3. F   4. T   5. T   6. F   7. T

H Fill in the Blanks

Teach the imperative form of the verb orally by having students go through the steps in washing clothes. (See Introduction, Action Sequence, page v.)
Answers: 1. Go   2. Put   3. Pick up   4. Read, Use   5. Pour   6. Pour   7. Sit, read

Expansion Exercises

Vocabulary

Measurements: Develop additional matching exercises with other measures such as $1/3$ cup, $3/4$ cup, teaspoon, tablespoon.

Clothing: Use the clothes orientation of the unit to teach clothing vocabulary. Have students name the items of clothing they are wearing. Then have students match word cards with pictures of clothing items. (See Introduction, Matching Pairs, page v.)

Reading

Directions with Measurements: Bring in directions from an assortment of products that use measurements, for example, cake mix, soap powder, soup. Have students work in pairs to scan the directions and then have them orally tell the class the measurements in the directions.

Clothing Labels: More advanced students can learn to read washing instructions on clothing labels. Have students sort a set of teacher-made labels (or labels on real clothes) into different categories, for example, wash by hand; wash colors separately; don't wash.

Closing Exercises

Map

The man lives at 5 Apple Road. Have students find his house on the map. If the washing machine is broken, the man will have to take his clothes to the ABC Laundry. Have students find it on the map and trace/describe the route from the man's house to the laundry.

What Do You Think?

Ask students: "You cannot read the directions on a box of detergent. What do you do?"

UNIT 2   911

Subject

Signs and Symbols, Using the Telephone, Household Safety, Storing Products

Situation

Drinking poison. A mother finds that her baby has drunk poison. *Last frame:* The mother gives her home address to the emergency operator.

Cultural Notes

In nonindustrial societies, the use of telephones is not common. Even in cultures where there are telephones, the concept of a telephone number to call in an emergency is not usual. In the U.S., many people keep a list of emergency telephone numbers by the phone. Also, using very toxic substances for household cleaning is not as common in nonindustrialized societies as it is in the U.S. Therefore students may not be aware of the need to store bottles containing these dangerous chemicals out of the reach of children.

Exercises

A Frames

Note: If the emergency number in the students' area is not 911, substitute the appropriate number in the story.

1. A baby sees a bottle of poison.
2. The baby drinks the poison.
3. The baby gets sick.
4. The baby falls down.
5. The baby's mother walks into the room. She is carrying a cup of coffee.
6. She sees the baby. She drops the cup of coffee. She screams.
7. She calls the emergency number 911.
8. A man answers. He asks, "Can I help you?" She says, "This is an emergency."
9. He asks, "What happened?" She says, "My baby drank poison."
10. He asks, "What is your address?" She says, "33 B Street."

B Sequencing

Answers: First column: 4, 2, 10, 3, 9. Second column: 8, 1, 5, 7, 6.

C Matching

Teach the past tense by having students tell the story in the past by pretending that the incident happened last week. As students tell the story, write the past tense forms of the verbs on the board.
Answers: 1. d, g   2. a, h   3. b, i   4. e, f   5. c, j

D Matching

Teach the vocabulary by having students match word cards and picture cards.
Answers: 1. b, g   2. d, f   3. a, h   4. c, e

E Listening

Teach addresses orally by writing five to seven addresses on the board. Read an address aloud and have individual students point to the one read.

Script:

1. He lives at 33 C Street.
2. She lives at 14 Circle Street.
3. They live at 16 16th Avenue.
4. She lives at 50A Ram Drive.
5. He lives at 24 14th Street.
6. She lives at 7 N Avenue.
7. They live at 15 Green Drive.
8. They live at 10 Second Street.

9. She lives at 61 Main Street.
10. He lives at 108 80th Street.
11. They live at 19 First Street.
12. She lives at 3 Green Drive.
13. She lives at 44 Third Street.
14. He lives at 72 Seventh Street.
15. They live at 33 A Street.

Answers: 1. b   2. a   3. a   4. a   5. b   6. c   7. a   8. a   9. c   10. a   11. c   12. a   13. b   14. c   15. c

F True/False

Answers: 1. F   2. T   3. F   4. T   5. T   6. T   7. T

G Fill in the Blanks

Answers: 1. saw   2. drank   3. fell   4. saw   5. screamed   6. dropped   7. called   8. asked   9. drank   10. address

Expansion Exercises

Grammar

Verb Tenses: Have students use the action verbs in this story to retell the story in the present continuous tense. For example, "The baby is drinking poison." Then have students practice using the future tense to tell what is going to happen next. For example, "The ambulance is going to take the baby to the hospital."

Listening/Speaking

Dialogue: Have pairs of students practice the dialogue between the mother and the emergency operator. Then ask for a few volunteers to perform the dialogue in front of the class using toy telephones.

Reading

Telephone List: Provide students with a local-number telephone list of the people in Exercise D.

Example: POLICE   254-5567
Example: FIRE DEPARTMENT   246-8879

Ask students, "What's the number of the police?"

Writing

Addresses: Have students tell their own addresses to the class. Have the other students write what they hear. Use this activity as an opportunity to practice clarification skills. For example, Student A: "My address is 13 Main Street." Student B: "13 or 30?" Student C: "How do you spell "Main"?"

Closing Exercises

Map

This incident takes place at 33 B Street. Have students locate the address on the map. Have the students find the hospital and ask them to trace/describe the route an ambulance might follow from the hospital to the house.

Role-Play

Emergency Calls: Prepare a set of picture cards that illustrate various emergency situations, for example, a kitchen fire, a badly cut finger. Put the cards face down. Have a student pick a card, look at it, run to a (toy) telephone and make a call to 911 to report the emergency. The teacher (or a more advanced student) can play the role of the emergency operator.

What Do You Think?

Ask students: "What will probably happen next in the story?" "Where should you keep the poison (or other dangerous items)?"

UNIT 3   CHECKOUT COUNTER

Subject

Shopping for Food

Situation

Checking out at a supermarket. A woman removes items one by one from her shopping basket, including her baby. *Last frame:* She takes her baby and pays the bill.

Cultural Notes

In some cultures shopping is in open-air markets without fixed prices. The concept of a large supermarket with prepackaged products, checkout lines, shopping carts with seats for small children and a cash register with a price scanner that enters item prices one at a time may be unfamiliar to students from these cultures.

Exercises

A Frames

1. A woman puts a carton of milk on the counter. She is going to put down a box of tea.
2. She puts down the box of tea. She is going to put down a can of soup.
3. She puts down the can of soup. She is going to put down a carton of eggs.
4. She puts down the carton of eggs. She is going to put down a bottle of juice.
5. She puts down the bottle of juice. She is going to put down a bag of rice.
6. She puts down the bag of rice. She is going to put down a jar of coffee.
7. She puts down the jar of coffee. She is going to put down her baby.
8. The baby is on the counter. The cashier is surprised. The woman looks in her basket for her baby.
9. The woman is embarrassed.
10. She takes the baby and pays the bill.

B Sequencing

Answers: First column: 8, 2, 3, 1, 5.   Second column: 9, 6, 10, 4, 7.

C Matching

Teach vocabulary by showing a variety of foods packaged in different containers. Have students name the items and the containers. Have students match a word card for the food/container with the item.
Answers: 1. f, bag   2. e, can   3. d, box   4. b, jar   5. a, carton   6. c, bottle

D Matching

Introduce new vocabulary by showing the items and containers. Have students name them and then match item and word cards.
Answers: 1. d, pound   2. b, bag   3. e, head   4. c, bag   5. a, bunch

E Game

Teach food vocabulary by showing food items and containers and having students identify them. Teach prices by writing five to seven prices on the board. Point to a price and have individual students read it. Then have students play the game. (See Introduction, Play the Game, page v.)

F True/False

Answers: 1. F   2. T   3. T   4. F   5. T   6. T   7. T

G Fill in the Blanks

Answers: 1. carton   2. box   3. can   4. carton   5. bottle   6. bag   7. jar   8. puts
9. counter   10. baby

Expansion Exercises

Vocabulary

Containers: Bring in a variety of supermarket items. Have students separate the items by the kind of container. For example, carton: milk, juice, eggs; can: soup, juice, vegetable.

Grammar

Count/Non-Count Nouns: Have students separate the story items into count/non-count categories. For example, rice: non-count, bananas: count.

Reading

Prices: Prepare number cards with different prices (for example, $1.50, .25, 45¢). Give each student a card. Call out an amount of money. The student who has the card raises his hand.

Writing

Prices: Give students a worksheet that lists item, unit price and quantity purchased. Have students compute the cost and the total.

Example:

ITEM	UNIT PRICE	QUANTITY	COST
rice	$1.20/lb.	5 lbs.	_____
carrots	$ .59/lb.	3 lbs.	_____
		TOTAL	_____

Closing Exercises

Map

The supermarket is on Orange Street. Have students locate it on the map. The woman lives at 25 Bank Street. Have students trace/describe the route she takes to get to the supermarket.

Role-Play

Arrange the room as a store using desks as shelves and checkout counters. Put food pictures with prices on the shelves. Assign a few students to be cashiers; the others will be shoppers. Give pairs of shoppers a shopping list (items can be shown in pictures or words depending on class level) and play money. Shoppers find the pictures of the food on the shelves to match their lists. They take the food pictures to the checkout counter. Clerks add up the total and shoppers pay the bill. Clerks make change as appropriate.

What Do You Think?

Ask the students: "You are given the wrong change at a store. What do you do?"

UNIT 4   DR. LEE

Subject

Health Services, Doctor/Patient Relationships, Male/Female Relationships

Situation

Visiting a doctor's office. A man finds out that Dr. Lee is a woman, and he does not want to take off his pants in front of her. *Last frame:* The man is embarrassed when the woman doctor examines him.

Cultural Notes

In some cultures, male patients would never be examined by a female doctor. In the U.S., however, female doctors see both male and female patients. In the U.S., gender is not a consideration in the professional relationship between doctor and patient.

In some cultures, appointments to see a doctor are not necessary. In the U.S., not only are appointments often necessary, but if not cancelled in advance, the patient may have to pay.

Exercises

A Frames

1. A man goes to a clinic.
2. The receptionist asks, "Do you have an appointment?" The man answers, "Yes, with Dr. Lee." He shows his appointment card.
3. The doctor says, "Sit down, please." The doctor is a woman. The man is surprised.
4. She says, "Take off your shirt." He says, "OK."
5. He takes off his shirt.
6. She says, "Take off your pants." He says, "No."
7. She says again, "Take off your pants." He says, "OK."
8. He takes off his pants. The doctor says, "OK."
9. The doctor says, "Lie down here." He covers his face.
10. He lies down on the table. She listens to his heart. The man is embarrassed.

B Sequencing

Answers: First column: 7, 1, 10, 4, 3. Second column: 6, 8, 9, 2, 5.

C Matching

Answers: 1. c   2. e   3. a   4. b   5. f   6. g   7. d

D Listening

Teach days and dates by saying a day or date and having students point to it on a calendar. Then teach time by saying a time and having students set the hands on a cardboard clock. Introduce the concept of an appointment card by drawing a large, completed appointment card on the board. Ask questions about the card, for example, "What time is the appointment?" "Is it in the morning or afternoon?" Then erase the days, dates and times from the card on the board. Dictate days, dates and times and have individual students write them on the card on the board.

Script:

1. Mr. E. Lee has an appointment on Monday, May 10 at 9:00 a.m.
2. Ms. B. Brown has an appointment on Wednesday, July 26 at 4:00 p.m.
3. Mr. P. Brown has an appointment on Thursday, December 9 at 1:00 p.m.
4. Ms. K. Lee has an appointment on Tuesday, February 17 at 10:30 a.m.
5. Mr. G. Rice has an appointment on Friday, October 30 at 11:45 a.m.
6. Ms. N. Rice has an appointment on Tuesday, January 4 at 2:30 p.m.

E True/False

Answers: 1. T   2. F   3. F   4. F   5. T   6. T   7. T

F Fill in the Blanks

Answers: 1. appointment   2. goes   3. woman   4. Sit   5. Take   6. take   7. lies   8. listens

Expansion Exercises

Vocabulary

Body Parts/Illnesses: Teach the names of various parts of the body. Call out the name of a body part and have students point to that part of their body. Then by using mime or by showing pictures of various illnesses (headache, sore throat, a cold, a fever), teach words to describe the illness. For example, "I have a headache." "I have a fever."

Dialogue: Have students work in pairs to develop a dialogue describing illnesses, for example, Doctor: "What's the matter?" Patient: "I have a headache."

Grammar

Imperatives: Have students go through the steps in an examination by the doctor. (See Introduction, Action Sequence, page v.)

Reading

Appointment Cards: Make and give an appointment card to each student showing the student's name, a day, a date and a time. Make each card slightly different. Call out the information on the card (without saying the name of the student). Have the student with that information come to the front of the room with the card.

Closing Exercises

Map

The clinic is located on California Street. Have students find it on the map. The man lives next to the ABC Tool Co. Have students trace/describe the route he takes to the clinic. If the doctor prescribes medicine for the man, he will need to go to the pharmacy. Have students trace/describe his route from the clinic to the pharmacy on California Street.

What Do You Think?

Ask students: "The man arrives late for his appointment with the doctor. What do you think will happen?" "The man refuses to remove his pants and leaves the doctor's office. Will he have to pay for his appointment?"

UNIT 5   EXACT CHANGE

Subject

Transportation, U.S. Currency

Situation

Using exact change on buses. A man without the exact change for bus fare has to get off the bus to get change. *Last frame:* When the man gets back to the bus stop, the bus is gone.

Cultural Notes

Bus systems in many countries employ a person whose job is to move around the bus collecting fares and making change. In the U.S., many local bus systems use fare boxes that require exact change because of the danger of robberies and because bus drivers do not have time to make change while driving. Passengers can get exact change from a change machine before boarding a bus.

Exercises

A Frames

1. A man goes to the bus stop. The bus fare is 75 cents.
2. (He gets on the bus.) The bus driver tells him to use exact change. The man only has $1.00.
3. He gets off the bus.
4. He asks a woman on 3rd Street, "Do you have change?" She says, "No."
5. He asks a woman on Post Office Road, "Do you have change?" She says, "Go in the post office."
6. The man sees a change machine in the post office.
7. He puts a dollar in the change machine.
8. The change comes out. He gets 4 quarters.
9. He runs to the bus stop.
10. The bus is gone.

B Sequencing

Answers: First Column: 3, 5, 10, 4, 6. Second Column: 7, 9, 1, 2, 8.

C Matching

Answers: 1. c   2. e   3. a   4. g   5. f   6. d   7. b

D Listening

Teach money by using (play) coins and bills. Give small groups of students $5 to $10 worth of coins and bills. Call out an amount of money, for example: 75 cents. Groups work together to show the class 75 cents (3 quarters; 7 dimes and 1 nickel; 2 quarters, 2 dimes and a nickel). Then teach making change by giving groups of students $5 worth of play coins and bills. Show a coin or a bill. Students show change for that coin or bill. For example, T. shows a quarter. Students show 2 dimes and 1 nickel or 5 nickels.

Script:

1. Do you have change for a dollar?
2. Do you have change for a quarter?
3. Do you have change for a half dollar?
4. Do you have change for a dime?
5. Do you have change for five dollars?
6. Do you have change for ten dollars?

Answers: 1. b   2. a   3. a   4. b   5. c   6. a

E True/False

Review the past tense by having students tell the story as if it happened yesterday. As students tell the story, write the past tense of the verbs on the board.
Answers: 1. F   2. T   3. T   4. T   5. F   6. F   7. T

F Fill in the Blanks

Answers: 1. went   2. got   3. Put   4. got   5. change   6. Go   7. saw   8. put   9. quarters   10. ran

Expansion Exercises

Listening/Speaking

Requests: Teach polite requests. For example, "Excuse me. Do you have change/the time/a match?" "Excuse me. Where can I get change/a newspaper/a sandwich?" Demonstrate the exchange using visuals or real objects. Cue students with the visuals or real objects and have them practice the exchange in pairs.

Listening/Speaking

Dialogue: Have groups of four students develop and practice the dialogue between the man, the bus driver and the women on 3rd Street and Post Office Road. Then ask for one group to perform the dialogue in front of the class.

Grammar

Imperatives: Have students go through the steps of taking a bus. Then have them go through the steps in using a change machine. (See Introduction, Action Sequence, page v.)

Reading

Sight words: Post around the room signs commonly seen on buses: NO SMOKING, EXACT CHANGE, EXIT, PUSH, PULL FOR STOP, THESE SEATS RESERVED FOR THE ELDERLY AND HANDICAPPED. Teach these words by demonstrating the action or showing visuals. Then have students match the actions/visuals with the sight words.

Closing Exercises

Map

The bus stop is at the corner of 3rd Street and Post Office Road. Ask students to locate the bus stop, 3rd Street, Post Office Road, and the Post Office on the map. The man lives at 17 Bank Street. Have students describe/trace the route the man walks from his house to the bus stop.

Role-Play

Set up desks to represent seats on a bus. Post signs for BUS STOP, EXACT CHANGE, ENTRANCE, EXIT, NO SMOKING (and other sight words seen on buses and taught in class). Assign one student to be the driver. The other students are passengers. Give students different amounts of money (some receive change, some bills). When they board the bus, they must pay the exact amount or get off. If they don't have exact change, they can request change from their classmates.

What Do You Think?

Ask students: "Why do buses require exact change?" "How is U.S. public transportation different from public transportation in your country?"

UNIT 6   FOUR-DAY JOB

Subject

On-the-Job Responsibilities/Expectations, Workplace Rules and Policies

Situation

Applying for, getting and losing a job. A man gets a job in a grocery store, but one day he goes to work late. *Last frame:* He's looking for another job.

Cultural Notes

In some cultures, when a person is late, it is assumed there is a valid reason. In the U.S., however, if employees do not call in with a valid reason when they are going to be late, it is assumed they are not responsible. Losing a job because of lateness may affect a person's ability to get another job since potential employers may require references from former employers.

Exercises

A Frames

1. It's Monday. A man sees a Help Wanted sign at G & D Grocery.
2. He asks for a job. (He asks, "Do you have a job?") The manager asks him a lot of questions. The manager hires him.
3. It's Tuesday. He's working. (He's selling fish.)
4. It's Wednesday. He's working.
5. It's Wednesday night. He's drinking with friends (at Joe's Bar).
6. It's Thursday morning. It's 9:00 a.m. He's sleeping.
7. It's 11:00 a.m. He's getting up. He's holding his head. He has a headache.
8. He goes to work (to G & D Grocery). The manager says, "Out." ("You're fired.")
9. It's Friday. He's looking for a new job. He sees a HELP WANTED sign at M & N Grocery.
10. It's Saturday. He's looking for a new job. He sees a HELP WANTED sign at the Pharmacy.

B Sequencing

Answers: First column: 5, 3, 4, 6, 9. Second column: 10, 2, 1, 8, 7.

C Matching

Answers: 1. c   2. d   3. b   4. f   5. a   6. g   7. e

D Crossword Puzzle

Teach the abbreviations by calling out a day and having students point to the abbreviation on a calendar. Then have students match two sets of word cards: one set with the names of the days of the week, the other set with the abbreviations. Then have students complete the exercise. 1. Tuesday, 2. Saturday, 3. Thursday, 4. Sunday, 5. Monday.

E Game

Teach the concept of a time card by drawing one on the board and bringing in a sample if available. Fill out a sample time card and ask students to show you the name, day, time in and time out. Then ask students questions about the time card, for example: "What day is it?" "What time did the person leave?" Explain that many companies require employees to punch in and out with a time card. A person's pay is based on the number of hours shown on the time card. Then have students play the game. (See Introduction, Play the Game, page v.)

F True/False

Answers: 1. T   2. F   3. F   4. T   5. T   6. F   7. T

G Fill in the Blanks

Answers: 1. job   2. grocery   3. fish   4. store   5. bar   6. sleeps   7. late   8. angry   9. looks

Expansion Exercises

Vocabulary

Days of Week: Have students play three-in-a-row (see Introduction, Play the Game, page v) with names of days of the week in the boxes.

Reading/Writing

Sight Words: Make cards with sight words that are commonly seen on application forms, such as NAME, ADDRESS, OCCUPATION. Teach these sight words by pointing to a card and having individual students give the personal information required, for example, Teacher: (shows OCCUPATION card) Student A: "Secretary." Then have students practice filling out simple job application forms using the sight words. The application forms can then be used as the basis for job interview role-plays.

Listening/Speaking

Explaining: When a student arrives late to class, use this opportunity to teach language for explaining lateness or absence. Ask the student: "Why are you late?" Use the student's response to teach appropriate language. For example, "I'm sorry." "I'm sick." "My car won't start." Then have students practice making phone calls to a place of employment to explain sickness or lateness using the language they practiced. They should begin the conversation by asking for their boss, "May I speak to Ms. Lee?" The teacher or an advanced student can take the role of the employer.

Listening/Reading/Writing

Time Cards: Make time cards on 3x5 cards that include students' names, days of the week, times in and times out. Place the cards in a box. Have students take turns drawing a time card and reading the information to the class. Have other students write the information they hear.

Closing Exercises

Map

Ask students to locate the G & D Grocery where the man works, Joe's Bar where he goes for a drink, and the M & N Grocery and the Pharmacy where he goes to look for a new job. The man lives at 26 1st Street. Have students describe/trace the route he takes to get from his home to the G & D Grocery.

What Do You Think?

Ask students: "Do you think the boss should fire the man because he was late one time?"

UNIT 7   GAS

Subject

Household Safety

Situation

Using a gas stove. A woman turns on her gas stove, but she doesn't light it. *Last frame:* The gas in the house causes an explosion when the woman's husband lights a cigarette.

Cultural Notes

Students from nonindustrial societies or rural areas may not be familiar with Western appliances such as gas or electric stoves. Some gas stoves have a pilot light that automatically lights the stove when it's turned on. Other gas stoves need a match to light them. If burners are not turned off when the stove is not being used, the build-up of gas in the house can cause an explosion.

Exercises

A Frames

1. A woman turns on the gas stove.
2. The phone rings. She doesn't light the stove. (She doesn't turn off the gas.)
3. The woman goes to answer the phone. (The gas is on.)
4. The woman talks on the phone. (The gas is on.)
5. The woman hangs up the phone. (The gas is on.)
6. The woman sits down in the living room. (The gas is on.)
7. Her husband comes home. (The gas is on.)
8. The man takes out a cigarette.
9. The man lights a cigarette.
10. (There's a big explosion.) The house blows up.

B Sequencing

Answers: First column: 3, 4, 5, 1, 10. Second column: 7, 8, 9, 2, 6.

C Matching

Answers: 1. e   2. a   3. c   4. d   5. f   6. g   7. b

D Matching

Teach the vocabulary words by showing large cards of the pictures and the words. Have students match the cards.
Answers: 1. g   2. b   3. f   4. a   5. c   6. d   7. e

E Game

Do number 1 as a whole class. Point out that number 1 in Exercise D is number 1 in the Crossword Puzzle.

F True/False

Answers: 1. F   2. T   3. T   4. F   5. F   6. F   7. T

G Fill in the Blanks

Answers: 1. rings   2. answers   3. turn   4. hangs   5. sits   6. comes   7. cigarette   8. blows

Expansion Exercises

Grammar

Imperative: Bring in a picture of a gas stove. Have students go through the steps in using a gas stove. (See Introduction, Action Sequence, page v.)

Listening/Speaking

Phone Calls: Have students practice making an emergency phone call to 911. Have students use language such as, "This is an emergency. There's a fire at 19 Bank Street."

Vocabulary:

Appliances: Show pictures of different household appliances. Have students identify the pictures and name one of the uses, for example, toaster: make toast; stove: cook.

Reading:

Phone Directory: Give small groups of students a local phone directory and a worksheet with a list of emergency personnel to locate. Include Police, Fire Department, Ambulance, Hospital and the general emergency number. Have students find the numbers in the phone book and write them on the worksheet.

Closing Exercises

Map

The house in this story is located at 19 Bank Street. Have students find it on the map. Then have them trace/describe the route that the fire department or ambulance would take to get to the house.

What Do You Think?

Ask students: "What will happen next?" "You smell gas in your house. What do you do?"

UNIT 8   MIDNIGHT

Subject

Safety in the City, Neighborhoods

Situation

Walking alone late at night. At midnight a woman leaves work and walks several blocks alone to a bus stop. *Last frame:* A man who has approached the woman puts his arm around her.

Cultural Notes

Working the night shift and then traveling home late at night will be a new experience, especially for students from rural areas. Before students decide to walk alone at night they should consider several things: Are there other people around? Is the bus stop in sight? Are there any open stores nearby? Is the street well lit? There are some options other than walking alone: the woman could walk with a coworker, ride with a coworker, have someone pick her up at work, or take a taxi.

Exercises

A Frames

1. A woman looks at the clock. It's (almost) midnight. She turns off the machine.
2. She punches out.
3. She starts walking. (She walks between buildings number 8 and 10.)
4. She walks between number 12 and the ABC Tool Company.
5. She walks another block. (She walks between 16 and 18.)
6. She walks another block. (She walks between 20 and 22.)
7. She sees the bus stop.
8. She waits at the bus stop.
9. A man walks toward the bus stop.
10. He puts his arm around her. He says, "Hi." She's surprised.

B Sequencing

Answers: First column: 3, 1, 4, 9, 5. Second column: 8, 10, 7, 6, 2.

C Matching

Answers: 1. b   2. g   3. e   4. d   5. f   6. a   7. c

D Matching

Teach the safety sight words by showing large visuals of the symbols and large word cards of the vocabulary. Have students match words with the pictures.
Answers: 1. h   2. b   3. g   4. a   5. f   6. c   7. e   8. d

E Game

Have students play the game. (See Introduction, Play the Game, page v.)

F True/False

Answers: 1. T   2. T   3. F   4. T   5. T   6. T   7. F

G Fill in the Blanks

Answers: 1. works   2. midnight   3. turns   4. walks   5. bus   6. waits   7. man   8. arm

Expansion Exercises

Speaking/Reading

Directions: Draw a simple map on the board showing several streets with numbered/labeled buildings on them. Give a student a marker. Have the student move the marker according to your oral directions. For example, "Walk to the school." "Walk one block." "Walk between buildings 10 and 12."

Reading

Sight words: Make a visual of a bus showing the front with a bus number, for example: 12A. Make several other signs with bus numbers. Put different signs on the front of the bus visual. Have students practice reading the signs.

Reading

Bus Schedules: Make a simple bus schedule including a bus number and a destination (either the word or a picture). Ask students, "Which bus goes to the hospital?"

Example:

BUS	PLACE
5A	HOSPITAL
20C	SUPERMARKET

Closing Exercises

Map

The woman works at the Tip Top Box Company. The bus stop is in front of 22 Apple Road. Ask students to find Tip Top Box Company on the map. Then ask them to trace/describe her route from work to the bus stop.

UNIT 9   THE NEIGHBOR'S KITCHEN

Subject

Household Safety, Sanitation, Tenant/Landlord Responsibilities, Neighbors

Situation

Socializing informally at home. A woman invites a neighbor to her house for coffee. *Last frame:* The women are drinking coffee in a dirty, unsafe kitchen.

Cultural Notes

In some cultures it is uncommon to entertain guests in the kitchen or to visit someone without advance notice. In the U.S., however, it is not unusual to socialize informally with guests in the kitchen or to drop by for a visit without an advance invitation.

This story shows an extreme example of an unsanitary living environment. Some of the problems in this kitchen might result from lack of knowledge of Western technology. A kitchen as dirty and unsafe as this one is a health hazard. If the woman is renting, the landlord could require that she move out if she doesn't correct the problems. Some of these problems violate health codes and are a danger to other tenants.

Exercises

A Frames

1. A woman telephones her neighbor. (She lives in house number 11. Her neighbor lives in house number 13.)
2. She asks, "Do you want to come over for some coffee?" Her neighbor says, "OK".
3. The neighbor goes to the house. (It's number 11.) She knocks on the door.
4. Her friend says, "Come in."
5. They drink coffee in the kitchen. The kitchen is very dirty. Some problems are: There's water on the floor. There are flies in the garbage. There's a broken window. There's a knife on the floor.

B Sequencing

These 10 frames describe in detail how the woman invites her friend for coffee. Since the students have not seen these frames in order in Exercise A, consider demonstrating how the woman invites her friend for coffee first.
Answers: First column: 5, 7, 1, 9, 8. Second column: 2, 3, 6, 10, 4.

The Story Frames (in sequence):

 1. A woman telephones her neighbor. (She lives in house number 11.)
 2. She dials the number.
 3. The phone rings. (The neighbor lives in house number 13.)
 4. The neighbor picks up the phone.
 5. The woman says, "Hello." Her neighbor says, "Hi."
 6. She asks, "Do you want to come over for some coffee?" Her friend says, "OK."
 7. The neighbor goes to the house.
 8. She knocks on the door.
 9. Her friend opens the door. She says, "Come in."
10. The women drink coffee in the kitchen.

C Matching

Teach the names of kitchen appliances by showing pictures or actual items and having students match these pictures with word cards. Then teach prepositions of place by putting objects in various places in the classroom and having students describe the location. Students will use these prepositions to describe the location of the objects in Exercises D and E and to tell where to safely store dangerous household products.
Answers: 1. c, l   2. f, h   3. b, i   4. e, g   5. a, j   6. d, k

D Circle the Problems

The problems include: 1. The garbage can is not covered. 2. Garbarge is on the floor—not in bags and in the can. 3. There's water on the floor—the refrigerator probably needs to be defrosted. 4. There are flies and cockroaches around the garbage can.   5. The curtains above the stove are a possible fire hazard.   6. There's poison on the sink—not properly stored.   7. The coffee pot cord is within reach of the small child.   8. There's a hole in the kitchen window.   9. A bowl and knife are on the floor—the knife is a potential hazard for the child.   10. There are too many appliances plugged into one outlet.   11. Food is unstored and spilled on the counter.   12. Cockroaches are climbing up the cabinets.

E Listening

Teach prepositions of place by placing real objects or pictures (poison, a garbage can, a bowl, a coffee pot, and a table) in different locations in the room and orally describing their location (beside, in front of, behind, etc.). Describe various locations and have students place the objects according to your directions, for example, "The poison is beside the coffee pot." Then read the script and have students put the correct number in the box.

Script:

1. The poison is under the table.
2. The poison is in the garbage can.
3. The poison is beside the bowl.
4. The poison is between the coffee pot and the bowl.
5. The poison is on the table.
6. The poison is beside the garbage can.

Answers: First column: 5, 3. Second column: 2,1. Third column: 6, 4.

F Listening

Repeat the preparation for the above exercise using the vocabulary: knife, coffee pot, baby, bowl, table, poison.

Script:

1. The knife is next to the coffee pot.
2. The knife is between the baby and the bowl.
3. The knife is in front of the bowl.
4. The knife is on the table.
5. The knife is next to the poison.
6. The knife is under the table.

Answers: First column: 3, 6. Second column: 4, 1. Third column: 2, 5.

G True/False

Answers: 1. T   2. F   3. F   4. T   5. T   6. T   7. F

H Fill in the Blanks

Have students refer to the picture in Exercise D.
Answers: 1. in   2. on   3. over   4. behind   5. beside   6. next to   7. on   8. under

Expansion Exercises

Grammar

Imperative: Ask students to tell you how the problems in the kitchen can be corrected, for example, "Put the poison in the cabinet."

Grammar

Modals: Teach modals of possibility (may, might, could) by pointing to kitchen problems and making statements. Teacher (points to knife on floor): "What do you think will happen?" "The baby may cut himself." or "The baby might pick it up." Then give students pictures of the problems and have them practice making statements using may, might, could.

Listening/Speaking

Invitations: Teach the language for inviting and for refusing and accepting an invitation. For example, "Can you come to my house for coffee?", "Would you like to go to the movies?", "Yes, Thank you.", "No, I'm sorry. I can't. I have to work." Have students practice this language in pairs. Using toy telephones have Student A invite Student B to a social event. Show picture cards to cue the type of invitations, for example, coffee, dinner, a movie.

Listening/Speaking

Explaining/Requesting: Teach the language for explaining a problem and then making requests for services. For example, "My sink is leaking. Can you repair it?" "When can you come?" Have students practice this language by making a phone call to the landlord if they are tenants, to request that repairs be made, or, if they are homeowners, directly to a repair person.

Closing Exercises

Map

The two women live on Coffee Avenue. Have students locate the two houses on the map. If the woman wants to buy materials to repair her kitchen, she can go to the hardware store. Have students find it on the map and trace/describe her route from her house to the hardware store.

What Do You Think?

Ask students: "The woman is renting the apartment. Who is responsible for making each of the repairs?" "The landlord refuses to make repairs. What can the woman do?" "The woman refuses to clean her kitchen. What may happen?"

UNIT 10   NUMBERS

Subject

Numbers, Clarification: On the Job

Situation

Following oral instructions. A supervisor gives a man three tasks to complete: to take a box to a room at a certain time, to make copies of a paper, and to deliver the copies to another room. *Last frame:* The man is delivering the copies to the wrong room.

Cultural Notes

In some cultures, it is considered impolite to question a person in a supervisory position even to confirm or clarify information. In the U.S. employers expect employees to confirm or clarify.

Exercises

A Frames

This exercise is divided into two segments: a man delivering a box and a man making copies.

First Segment:

1. A supervisor says to an employee, "Take this box to Room 4 at 3:00." The employee says, "OK."
2. It's 4:00. The employee is carrying the box.
3. He takes the box to Room 3. A woman in Room 3 says, "Take this to Room 4."
4. He takes the box to Room 4. The man in Room 4 is angry. (It's late.)

Second Segment:

5. The supervisor says, "Make 19 copies." The employee says, "OK."
6. The employee puts the paper in the copy machine.
7. He counts the number of copies. . .20, 30, 40, 50, 60, 70, 80, 90. (He makes 90 copies.)
8. He takes the copies to his supervisor. He says, "(Here are) 90 copies." The supervisor shouts, "90?"
9. The supervisor tells the man to take 19 copies to Room 16. The man says, "OK."
10. The man takes all the copies to Room 60.

B Sequencing

Answers: First segment, First column: 3, 4. Second column: 1, 2. Second segment, First column: 3, 5, 1. Second column: 2, 4, 6.

C Matching

Answers: 1. b, 19   2. a, 4   3. g, 3   4. e, 60   5. d, 16   6. c, 90   7. f, 4:00

D Listening

Teach numbers orally by writing similar sounding numbers on the board, for example, 60, 16. Read a number and have individual students point to the number read.

Script:

1. ninety
2. eighty
3. thirteen
4. sixty
5. seventeen

6. fourteen
7. eight
8. fifteen
9. ninety
10. seventy

Answers: 1. b   2. a   3. b   4. b   5. b   6. a   7. a   8. b   9. b   10. b

E Game

Teach reading numbers by writing similar sounding numbers on the board, for example, 19, 90. Point to a number and have individual students read that number. Then have individual students (without pointing) read one of the two similar sounding numbers. Point to the number you hear. Have the student confirm/correct.

Teach time by setting a cardboard clock and asking individual students to tell you the time. Then write digital times on the board, point to a time and have individual students read the time. Then have students play the game. (See Introduction, Play the Game, page v.) Point out the direction in which the game moves by showing students how to follow the arrows. Then show students the ladders. Point out that when a student's marker lands on the top or bottom of a ladder, the student must follow the arrow either up or down.

F True/False

Answers: 1. F   2. F   3. T   4. T   5. T   6. T   7. T

G Fill in the Blanks

Answers: 1. room   2. supervisor   3. 19   4. copies   5. angry   6. Make   7. Take   8. 60

Expansion Exercises

Listening/Speaking

Clarification: Teach, students different ways to clarify unclear instructions ("Please repeat", "Where?", "Go to . . . ?", "The book?", "19 or 90?", "What should I do?") Ask a student to give you an instruction. Pretend that you don't understand and use one of the above clarification strategies. After demonstrating several, give individual students instructions very quickly and have them ask you for clarification.

Listening/Reading

Numbers: Write "problem" numbers (as in Exercise D) on the board. Divide the class into teams. The two teams line up in front of the board. Call out a number. One member from each team runs to the board and circles the number read. The first student to circle the number gets a point for his team.

Reading

Numbers: Have students play three-in-a-row (see Introduction, Play the Game, page v) with numbers; choose numbers for the board that are often confused.

Closing Exercises

Map

This story takes place at the "Daily Post" on B Street. Have students locate it on the map. The employee in this story lives at 18 Apple Road. Have students trace/describe his route from his home to his job.

What Do You Think?

Ask students: "What will the supervisor say/do next? What will the employee say/do?" "You are given unclear instructions at work in your country. What do you do?"

UNIT 11   ONE DAY'S WORK

Subject

Lifestyles, Male/Female Relationships

Situation

Reversing roles. A man works in the home; a woman works in a factory. *Last frame:* They're kissing.

Cultural Notes

In many cultures, it is unusual for women to work outside the home. In the U.S., many women raise families *and* work in jobs outside the home. Sometimes the woman works while the man stays at home and cares for the house and children. This may be a personal choice or because he can't find a job.

Exercises

A Frames

This story is divided into two segments: at home and at the factory.

First Segment:

1. It's 9:00 a.m. The husband is feeding the baby.
2. It's 11:00 a.m. He is washing the dishes.
3. It's 1:00 p.m. He is sweeping the floor.
4. It's 4:00 p.m. He is cooking dinner.

Second Segment:

5. It's 7:00 a.m. The wife is leaving the house. She is going to work. The husband is looking at their baby.
6. It's 8:00 a.m. The woman is punching in (at work).
7. It's 10:00 a.m. She is working (on an assembly line).
8. It's 2:00 p.m. She is taking a (coffee) break.
9. It's 5:00 p.m. She is punching out.
10. It's 6:00 p.m. The husband is reading the newspaper. They are kissing each other.

B Sequencing

Answers: First segment, First column: 3, 4. Second column: 2, 1. Second segment, First column: 5, 3, 1. Second column: 2, 6, 4.

C Matching

Teach time using cardboard clocks with movable hands. Write a digital time on the board and have pairs of students set their clocks to that time.
Answers: 1. b, j   2. a, m   3. d, i   4. f, h   5. g, l   6. e, k   7. c, n

D Game Vocabulary

Teach the vocabulary by having individual students mime different activities and other students tell what the student is doing. For example, Student A: (pretends to sweep the floor); Teacher: "What is he doing?" Student B: "He's sweeping the floor." Then have students match the action (or a picture of the action) with a word card describing the action.

E Game

Have students play the game. (See Introduction, Play the Game, page v.)

F True/False

Contrast the present and present continuous tenses by asking students questions, for example, "It's 10:00. What is he doing now? What does he do every day at 10:00?"
Answers: 1. F   2. T   3. F   4. F   5. F   6. T   7. T

G Fill in the Blanks

Answers: 1. works   2. feeds   3. washes   4. sweeps   5. cooks   6. reads   7. wife   8. factory
9. comes/goes   10. kisses

Expansion Exercises

Vocabulary

Daily Activities: Have students play Matching Pairs (see Introduction, Match the Picture . . . , page v) with pictures of daily activities on one set of cards and verbs to describe the activities on another set.

Grammar

Present Tense: Using pictures as cues, have students describe their everyday activities, for example, "At 7:00 I get up."

Grammar

Present Continuous Tense: Write (or draw pictures of) everyday activities on 3x5 cards. Have students draw a card and perform the action. Have other students guess what the action is.

Grammar

Past Tense: Write the verbs from the story on the board in the present continuous tense. Work with the regular past tense verbs first, then the irregular ones. Elicit the past tense form from the students by asking, "She's working now. What did she do yesterday?'" Then have students practice the past tense by taking the role of the husband or wife. Have them describe their day using the verbs from the story in the past tense. For example, Husband: "At 9:00 I fed the baby. Then I swept the floor."

Closing Exercises

Map

The man and woman live at 22 2nd Street. The factory where the woman works is the PKW Factory. Find the house and the worksite. Trace/describe the route that the woman takes to get from her house to work.

What Do You Think?

Ask students: "Would you like to be the man/woman in this story? Why? Why not?"

UNIT 12   PAY PHONE

Subject

Using the Telephone, Law and Police

Situation

Using a pay phone. A man leaves his suitcase outside a telephone booth while he makes a phone call. *Last frame:* Someone steals his suitcase.

Cultural Notes

In nonindustrialized countries, pay phones are not common. Students from these countries will not be familiar with their use. Coins (10 cents in some places; 25 cents in others) are needed in the U.S. to make a call from a pay phone. Telephones in a department store or office are for employees only. Therefore, pay phones are available in public areas such as the street and in the lobby and hallways of buildings. When using a pay phone, the caller should keep bags, suitcases, or parcels inside the telephone booth.

Exercises

A Frames

1. A man wants to find a phone. He's on Orange Street.
2. He goes to PG Department Store.
3. He asks the cashier, "Can I use your telephone?" She says, "No."
4. He goes outside. He sees a telephone booth.
5. He goes inside the telephone booth. He leaves his suitcase outside.
6. He takes out a quarter (25 cents).
7. He puts a quarter (25 cents) in the pay phone.
8. He dials the number.
9. A thief sees his suitcase.
10. The thief takes his suitcase.

B Sequencing

Answers: First column: 4, 2, 10, 5, 9. Second column: 6, 7, 1, 3, 8.

C Matching

Answers: 1. c   2. d   3. e   4. g   5. a   6. b   7. f

D Listening

Teach how to read phone numbers. Write a number on the board and point out that phone numbers in the U.S. almost always contain seven digits. Read the number showing that each number is usually read individually and that there is a pause after the first three numbers. Write several phone numbers that contain similar digits on the board. Read a number aloud and have individual students point to the number you read.

Script:

1. 346-6798
2. 256-7685
3. 445-5846
4. 563-3424
5. 466-6998
6. 643-2345
7. 743-2435

Answers: 1. b   2. a   3. c   4. a   5. c   6. b   7. b

E Listening

Teach the concept of area codes by asking a few students to tell you their phone numbers. Then write your local area code in front of the numbers. Show the area code map in the front of the phone book. Ask students: "Do you have a friend in Massachusetts/California?" "What city?" Have students find the state/city on the area code map and read you the area code. Write the area code for that section of the country on the board. Also point out that 800 area codes are toll-free numbers usually connected with a business or a service. Then write several telephone numbers on the board with some of the numbers missing. Ask individual students to fill in the blanks with the numbers you read.

Script:

1. 617-546-8711
2. 512-395-6815
3. 413-777-8395
4. 202-237-4728
5. 800-443-6679
6. 802-364-5757
7. 212-443-8691
8. 415-394-9562

F True/False

Answers: 1. F   2. T   3. F   4. T   5. T   6. T   7. T

G Fill in the Blanks

Answers: 1. looks   2. goes   3. use   4. pay   5. booth   6. suitcase   7. quarter   8. number
9. thief

Expansion Exercises

Grammar

Imperative: Have students go through the steps in using a pay phone. (See Introduction, Action Sequence, page v.)

Listening/Speaking

Polite Requests: Have students practice making polite requests based on the language in the story: "Excuse me. Can I use your phone?" Ask a student: "Can I use your pen?" Then show picture cue cards, for example, pencil, pen, car, radio, and have Student A practice making requests to Student B. Student B can decide to honor or refuse the request by responding, "Yes, you can.'" or "No. I'm sorry, you can't."

Reading/Listening

Phone Numbers: Have students write their own phone numbers on 3x5 cards. Then have them exchange phone number cards with a partner and read aloud the phone number of their partner. The other student verifies that the number is read correctly.

Reading/Writing

Phone Directories: Give students a worksheet with the names of individuals, professionals and businesses from the white pages of the local phone book. Divide students into small groups. Give each group a phone book. Have each group work together to find the numbers in the phone book and to write them on the worksheet.

Closing Exercises

Map

This story takes place on Orange Street. Have students locate Orange Street and the PG Department Store. The man wants to go to the police station to report the robbery. Have students trace/describe his route.

What Do You Think?

Ask students: "What will happen next? Who will the man call?" "Where should you put your suitcase/bag when you use a pay phone?"

UNIT 13   PICKLES

Subject

Shopping for Food, Shopping Etiquette

Situation

Sampling food at a supermarket. A woman samples a pickle from a jar on a supermarket shelf. *Last frame:* The manager tells the woman that she must pay for the jar of pickles.

Cultural Notes

In many countries shopping is mainly in markets where customers can sample food items before buying. In U.S. supermarkets most food is packaged either in plastic (meat, vegetables, fruit, bread) or in cans or jars. Sampling packaged or unpackaged food in U.S. supermarkets is not allowed except at deli counters where free samples are sometimes given.

Exercises

A Frames

1. A woman goes to a supermarket.
2. The woman walks down Aisle 3.
3. She sees a jar of pickles. (She doesn't know what it is.)
4. She opens the jar.
5. She takes out a pickle.
6. She tastes the pickle.
7. She spits it out. (She doesn't like it.)
8. She puts the pickle back in the jar.
9. She puts the lid back on the jar of pickles. The manager sees her.
10. The manager is angry. He tells her to pay for the pickles.

B Sequencing

Answers: First column: 3, 7, 2, 4, 6. Second column: 8, 9, 1, 10, 5.

C Matching

Answers: 1. f   2. a   3. b   4. j   5. h   6. c   7. g   8. d   9. i   10. e   11. l   12. k

D Game

Teach the food on the shopping list by showing the items. Mark off the classroom floor into aisles. Label each aisle according to the supermarket grid in the Supermarket Game (1A, 1B, 2A, 2B, etc.). Call out an aisle number, for example, 3A. Ask individual students to go to the aisle you call out. Then place food items in different locations on the aisles. Ask students to find an item and tell where the item is located. For example, Teacher: "Where's the fish?" Student A: "Aisle 3A." Have students play the game. (See Introduction, Play the Game, page v.)

E True/False

Have students tell the story orally in the past. As the students tell the story, write the past tense of the verbs on the board. Then point to individual verbs and have students read the words aloud.
Answers: 1. F   2. T   3. F   4. F   5. T   6. F   7. T

F Fill in the Blanks

Write the verbs from the picture story frames on the board. Write the regular verbs first (walk, open, taste, like). Have students change them to past tense by adding "ed" or "d". Then write the irregular verbs (go, see, take, spit, put, be, tell) and have students write the irregular past form next to the infinitive.

Answers: 1. saw 2. opened 3. opened 4. took 5. tasted 6. tasted 7. spit 8. saw 9. pickles.

Expansion Exercises

Vocabulary

Food: Bring in pictures of food items and have students divide the food by sections, for example, Produce, Meat, Bread, by putting the food under signs for each section.

Vocabulary

Senses—Taste: Bring in food items (or pictures) and ask, "What is this? How does it taste?" Teach students common vocabulary to describe the tastes of different foods: sweet, sour, bitter, hot, spicy, bland, etc. Bring in a few food items that students have probably not tasted before and have students taste them and describe the flavor using the vocabulary above.

Grammar

Imperative: Describe in a series of steps how to taste a pickle, beginning with "Open the jar." (See Introduction, Action Sequence, page v.)

Reading

Directions: Use chalk to mark off the classroom floor into aisles in a supermarket. Write aisle numbers (such as 2A, 4B) in the aisles. Give the students a series of oral directions to follow. For example, "Go to Aisle 3." "Go straight, turn right." "Go to the second aisle." Then have students give each other directions.

Closing Exercises

Map

The supermarket is on Orange Street. Have students locate it on the map and describe the route the woman will take from her home at 4 Coffee Avenue to get to the supermarket.

Role-Play

Divide students into groups of two. Have one student be the woman and the other the manager. Have students develop a role-play based on the story and conclude with the woman apologizing and explaining her action to the manager.

What Do You Think?

Ask students: "Should the woman pay for the pickles?" "Why are so many things in U.S. supermarkets in a package (plastic wrap, can, bottle, bag)?"

UNIT 14   THE SHOWER

Subject

Tenant/Landlord Responsibilities, Household Maintenance

Situation

Taking a shower. While taking a bucket bath, a man splashes water which leaks into the downstairs apartment. *Last frame:* The downstairs tenant tells the man to use the shower curtain.

Cultural Notes

In many countries bathrooms have drains in the floors so splashing water on the floor is acceptable. There are no floor drains in U.S. bathrooms so people use a shower curtain to keep the water inside the bathtub. Tenants may have to pay for any damage resulting from inappropriate use of a bathtub (or any household appliance).

Exercises

A Frames

1. A man goes into the bathroom. He carries a bucket.
2. He sits on the side of the bathtub. He turns on the faucet. He fills the bucket with water.
3. He takes a bath. He splashes water on the floor.
4. He pours water from the bucket. He splashes more water on the floor.
5. He dries himself with a towel. There's a lot of water on the floor.

6. The water leaks from apartment 3A to apartment 2A.
7. The neighbor in apartment 2A wakes up. The water leaks on him.
8. The neighbor is angry. He goes upstairs.
9. He points at the wet floor.
10. The neighbor shows the man how to use the shower curtain.

B Sequencing

Answers: First column: 3, 8, 7, 2, 1. Second column: 6, 5, 9, 4, 10

C Matching

Teach the present continuous tense by asking individual students to mime the actions in the different frames. Have other students tell what the student is doing: Student A: (turns on water). Teacher: "What is he doing?" Student B: "He's turning on the water." Then have the students tell the story as if it were happening right now.
Answers: 1. c   2. a   3. g   4. f   5. b   6. d   7. e

D Game Vocabulary

Show toy bathroom furniture or a visual of a bathroom with furnishings. Make word cards with the names of the bathroom furnishings. Have students match the word cards to the furnishings.

E Game

Have students play the game. (See Introduction, Play the Game, page v.)

F True/False

Answers 1. F   2. T   3. T   4. F   5. T   6. T   7. T

G Fill in the Blanks

Answers: 1. bucket   2. bathtub   3. water   4. bath   5. floor   6. apartment   7. upstairs
8. angry   9. shower

Expansion Exercises

Vocabulary

Bathroom: Provide students with pictures of items in the bathroom on one set of cards and the words on the other set. For more advanced students, other common words associated with the bathroom can be added, for example, toilet paper, wash cloth, mirror, soap, toothbrush, toothpaste. Then have students play Matching Pairs. (See Introduction, page v.)

Grammar

Imperatives: Go through the steps in taking a bath (shower or bucket bath). (See Introduction, Action Sequence, page v.)

Listening/Speaking

Apologies: Have students practice making an apology. Perform several actions that demand an apology: for example, step on someone's foot; knock a student's book on the floor; spill some water. After performing each action, apologize by using appropriate language, such as, "I'm sorry." "Excuse me." Then have students practice apologies in pairs.

Listening/Speaking

Dialogue: Have students in pairs develop a dialogue where Student A is the man in the bath and Student B is the angry neighbor. Have Student A apologize/explain to Student B.

Closing Exercises

Map

This story takes place at J's Apartments. Have students find it on the map. If the man needs to repair the water damage, he can get supplies at the hardware store. Have students trace/describe the route from his apartment to the hardware store.

What Do You Think?

Ask the students: "The man is renting the apartment. Who will have to pay for the damage?" "You are the tenant in apartment 3A. What do you say to the angry tenant in the downstairs apartment?"

UNIT 15   SMALL FIRE

Subject

On-the-Job Responsiblities, Safety

Situation

Reacting to an emergency on the job. While working, a man notices a small fire. Although there's a fire extinguisher on the wall, he runs downstairs to tell his boss. *Last frame:* The fire is no longer small.

Cultural Notes

In nonindustrial societies, electrical machines and chemical fire extinguishers may be uncommon. Students from these cultures may not know what to do in the event of an emergency with these machines. Also in some cultures the boss is responsible for any problem. In the U.S., employees are expected to know the proper procedure for an emergency and to take initiative in the event of emergencies.

Exercises

A Frames

1. A man works in a factory. He sews clothes. There's a fire extinguisher on the wall.
2. A small fire starts. He sees it.
3. He is afraid.
4. He starts running.
5. He runs downstairs from the 6th floor to the 5th floor.
6. He runs downstairs from the 5th floor to the 4th floor.
7. He tells the manager about the fire.
8. They run upstairs from the 4th floor to the 5th floor.
9. They run upstairs from the 5th floor to the 6th floor.
10. There's a big fire.

B Sequencing

Answers: First column: 10, 6, 2, 8, 1. Second column: 9, 4, 5, 7, 3.

C Matching

Answers: 1. g   2. d   3. f   4. b   5. a   6. c   7. e

D Matching

Teach vocabulary by posting the safety-related sight words around the room. Call out the sight words and ask individual students to point to those you say. Ask students where they have seen these signs, for example, on buses, in buildings, at the workplace. Describe situations and have students point to the appropriate sign, for example, Teacher: "You want to leave a building. Which sign do you look for?" Students: (point to EXIT).
Answers: 1. c   2. e   3. b   4. a   5. h   6. d   7. f   8. g

E Game

Have students play the game. (See Introduction, Play the Game, page v.)

F True/False

Answers: 1. T   2. F   3. T   4. F   5. F   6. T   7. T

G Fill in the Blanks

Answers: 1. man   2. sews   3. fire   4. fire   5. scared   6. downstairs   7. run   8. big

Expansion Exercises

Vocabulary

Occupations: Teach the names of different jobs. Ask students what job the man in the story has. Ask them to identify other jobs in this kind of company. Ask students what jobs they have. Show pictures of common occupations and have students point to and/or name their job or one they would like to have.

Vocabulary

Safe/Unsafe Work Conditions: Bring in pictures of people working, safely, and unsafely. Have students divide the pictures into two groups: one group shows safe working conditions; one shows unsafe working conditions. Have more advanced students describe the unsafe working conditions, for example, man running on wet floor; man not wearing a hard hat in a construction zone; woman in a food service not covering her hair.

Reading

Numbers: Draw a factory building with 10 floors. Label the floors 1st to 10th. Call out a number. Ask students to point to the floor with that number. Then point to a floor and have individual students tell you the floor number.

Listening/Speaking

Phone Calls: Teach appropriate language for emergency phone calls, for example, "This is an emergency. There's a fire at Pee Wee Clothing Factory. The address is. . . ." Have students practice making an emergency phone call to the Fire Department to report the fire.

Closing Exercises

Map

This incident takes place at the Pee Wee Clothing Factory. Ask students to locate it on the map. Have students locate the Fire Station and trace/describe the quickest route to the factory from the Fire Station. The man lives at 11 Post Office Road. Trace/describe his route to work.

Role-Play

Emergencies at Work: Have small groups of students develop a role-play for this picture story. Have one group perform the story exactly as shown in the picture story. Have another change the ending so the man immediately calls the fire department and then notifies the manager. Have a third group show what would happen if the man had used the fire extinguisher immediately. Ask students which ending they prefer.

What Do You Think?

Ask students: "What happens next?" "You are working in your own country. A fire starts. What do you do?"

UNIT 16 THE WRONG MESSAGE

Subject

Using the Telephone, Taking Messages, Clarifying Instructions

Situation

Taking telephone messages. A man takes a phone message incorrectly twice. *Last frame:* The man who gave the message waits for his friend to arrive.

Cultural Notes

In nonindustrialized societies, telephones are not common. Even students accustomed to using telephones will have problems taking messages over the phone, because it is more difficult to understand when not speaking face to face. In the U.S., people taking phone messages are expected to write them down and to repeat the information to insure accuracy.

Exercises

A Frames

1. It's Monday. A woman and a man are talking on the phone. The woman says, "Tell my friend to meet me at the school on Bank Street at 9:00 a.m." The man says, "OK".
2. The man tells the woman's friend to go to the bank on School Street at 9:00 a.m. (The message is not correct.) The friend says, "OK".
3. The friend goes to the bank on School Street. He waits but no one comes.
4. The woman goes to the school on Bank Street. She waits but no one comes.
5. It's Tuesday. The woman and the man are talking on the phone again. She asks, "Did you give the message to my friend?" The man says, "Yes."
6. She asks, "Are you sure?" He shouts, "Yes!"
7. She says again, "Tell my friend to go to the school on Bank Street at 9:00 a.m." The man says, "OK".
8. The man tells the woman's friend to go to the school on Bank Street at 9:00 p.m. (The message is not correct.) The friend says, "OK".

9. The woman goes to the school on Bank Street at 9:00 a.m. She waits but no one comes.
10. The man goes to the school on Bank Street at 9:00 p.m. He waits but no one comes.

B Sequencing

Answers: 1st column: 2, 3, 6, 10, 7. 2nd column: 4(9), 8, 5, 9(4), 1.

C Matching

Answers: 1. b   2. g   3. c   4. e   5. f   6. d   7. a

D Listening

Teach places, times and days. Write digital times on the board including a.m. and p.m. Read a time and have individual students point to the time read. Then have students set a cardboard clock with movable hands to that time. Put up a calendar in the classroom or write days of the week on the board. Call out a day and have students point to that day. Write several place names on the board or show pictures of various places in a town. Call out the name of a place and ask individual students to point to that word or picture.

Script:

    1. Meet me on School Street at 5:30 p.m. on Tuesday.
    2. Meet me on 9th Street at 1:00 p.m. on Sunday.
    3. Meet me on A Street at 8:15 a.m. on Monday.
    4. Meet me on D Street at 9:00 a.m. on Saturday.
    5. Meet me on 8th Street at 1:15 p.m. on Thursday.
    6. Meet me on Bank Street at 11:00 a.m. on Wednesday.

Answers: 1. b, c, b   2. c, a, c   3. a, a, b   4. c, a, c   5. a, b, a   6. b, c, c

E Game

Have students play the game. (See Introduction, Play the Game, page v.) After students have played the game and written the information in the box, ask students to tell the place, day and time that they wrote in their boxes.

F True/False

Answers: 1. T   2. T   3. F   4. F   5. T   6. T   7. T

G Fill in the Blanks

Answers: 1. gives   2. message   3. bank   4. goes   5. 9:00   6. woman   7. friend   8. shouts
9. school   10. p.m.

Expansion Exercises

Vocabulary

Places: Teach the names of places in a town, for example; bank, supermarket, pharmacy. Using the map in the front of the book, have students point out different places. Then have students practice telling each other where to meet, for example, "Meet me at the post office." The students who receive the information must touch the appropriate place on the map.

Listening/Speaking/Writing

Messages: Put up a partition separating two toy telephones or have students sit back to back. Students take turns practicing taking messages. Give Student A a card with a time and place written on it. Student A gives Student B the message. Student B listens to the message and writes it down. For example, Student A: (reading from card with "9:00 a.m., school" written on it) "Meet me at the school at 9:00 a.m." Student B: (writes: "school, 9:00 a.m.") When students don't understand they should ask for clarification, by saying, "Please repeat." or "I'm sorry. I didn't understand."

Closing Exercises

Map

Have students locate the bank on School Street and the school on Bank Street on the map. The woman lives at 24 3rd Street. The man lives at 16 Apple Road. Have students trace/describe the route they will take to get to the meeting places.

What Do You Think?

Ask students: "What do you think will happen next?"